FusionCharts
Beginner's Guide

The official guide for FusionCharts Suite

Create interactive charts in JavaScript (HTML5) and Flash
for your web and enterprise applications

Sanket Nadhani

Shamasis Bhattacharya

Pallav Nadhani

BIRMINGHAM - MUMBAI

FusionCharts
Beginner's Guide

The official guide for FusionCharts Suite

First published: April 2011

Production Reference: 1170412

Published by Packt Publishing Ltd.
Livery Place
35 Livery Street
Birmingham B3 2PB, UK.

ISBN 978-1-84969-176-5

www.packtpub.com

Cover Image by Quirk Brand Communication (hello@quirk.co.in)

Credits

Authors
Sanket Nadhani
Shamasis Bhattacharya
Pallav Nadhani

Reviewers
Adit Gupta
Karoline Osaland Klever

Acquisition Editor
Wilson D'souza

Lead Technical Editor
Shreerang Deshpande

Technical Editor
Unnati Shah

Project Coordinator
Sai Gamare

Proofreader
Kevin McGowan

Indexer
Tejal Daruwala

Graphics
Manu Joseph

Production Coordinator
Melwyn D'sa

Cover Work
Melwyn D'sa

About the Authors

Sanket Nadhani previously headed Marketing and Sales at FusionCharts, fresh out of college. As part of the role, he had to conceptualize different dashboards and demos and was often frustrated with the lack of practical resources on data visualization to learn from. Once he learned them after his daily bouts with tons of data, he started writing about the usability and best practices on the FusionCharts blog that have been well received.

He loves food, beer, and travelling. You can follow him on Twitter at `http://twitter.com/sanketnadhani`.

I want to thank the wonderful web community for sharing all their learning and experiences so selflessly. A lot of what I know and do today is because of you guys.

Shamasis Bhattacharya has been a part of FusionCharts since 2008. As a JavaScript architect, he heads the JavaScript development team and spends most of his time analyzing, modeling, and coding the FusionCharts JavaScript charting library with attention to smart software design and innovative data visualization countenances.

He writes on his blog `http://www.shamasis.net/` and spends the rest of his time with his wife, Madhumita.

My part in this book wouldn't have been worth reading had my wife not been around helping me and had not Pallav e-mailed me questioning whether I had been smoking while writing the draft!

Pallav Nadhani is the co-founder and CEO of FusionCharts, and an angel investor. He started FusionCharts at the age of 17 as a way to make pocket money. Today, FusionCharts has around 20,000 customers and 400,000 users in over 110 countries. His entrepreneurial journey has been covered by various magazines such as Forbes, Entrepreneur, Business Today, Economic Times, and numerous blogs and websites. He holds a Masters in Computer Science from The University of Edinburgh and loves traveling, beer, and poker.

He has also worked on the book "*Flash.NET*", *Friends of Ed Publication*.

I want to dedicate this book to Mom, who has always been my inspiration, and Puja, who has been my cheerful support throughout. I would also like to thank the entire FusionCharts team for taking FusionCharts to where it is today, and Hrishikesh for helping me with this book.

About the Reviewer

Karoline Osaland Klever works as a Senior Developer and Consultant at Epinova, focusing on web development with EPiServer and integrations with Microsoft Dynamics CRM. She was honored as one of the top three computer science students in Norway the year she graduated from the university and has, since then, released an open source framework for integration with Microsoft Dynamics CRM. She lives in Oslo, Norway.

www.PacktPub.com

Support files, eBooks, discount offers and more

You might want to visit www.PacktPub.com for support files and downloads related to your book.

Did you know that Packt offers eBook versions of every book published, with PDF and ePub files available? You can upgrade to the eBook version at www.PacktPub.com and as a print book customer, you are entitled to a discount on the eBook copy. Get in touch with us at service@packtpub.com for more details.

At www.PacktPub.com, you can also read a collection of free technical articles, sign up for a range of free newsletters and receive exclusive discounts and offers on Packt books and eBooks.

http://PacktLib.PacktPub.com

Do you need instant solutions to your IT questions? PacktLib is Packt's online digital book library. Here, you can access, read and search across Packt's entire library of books.

Why Subscribe?

- Fully searchable across every book published by Packt
- Copy and paste, print and bookmark content
- On demand and accessible via web browser

Free Access for Packt account holders

If you have an account with Packt at www.PacktPub.com, you can use this to access PacktLib today and view nine entirely free books. Simply use your login credentials for immediate access.

Table of Contents

Preface

As web developers, we build applications that feed on data. We parse it, process it, and report it. Our reports take the form of tables, grids, and diagrams such as charts, gauges, and maps. Parsing and processing are backend tasks that are invisible to the user. The actual reporting of data, however, is a bulk of an experience a user has with our application.

This book is a practical step-by-step guide to using FusionCharts Suite to create delightful web reports and dashboards. After creating your first chart in 15 minutes, you will learn advanced reporting capabilities such as drill-down and JavaScript integration. Finally, you round up the experience by learning reporting best practices including the right chart type selection and practical usability tips to become the data visualization guru among your peers.

What this book covers

Chapter 1, Introducing FusionCharts, introduces you to FusionCharts Suite and teaches you how to build your first chart in under 15 minutes. You will learn the XML and JSON data formats that FusionCharts Suite supports, and apply it to build different types of charts.

Chapter 2, Customizing your Chart, brings to you the wide spectrum of customization options you have with FusionCharts Suite, both aesthetically and functionally. You will learn how to customize the chart background and font, control how numbers appear on the chart, and add more context to charts using trendlines.

Chapter 3, JavaScript Capabilities, familiarizes you with the JavaScript programmability of FusionCharts Suite. Using them, you will be able to develop rich and interactive features around your charts and also learn ways to integrate FusionCharts with your web applications.

Chapter 4, Enabling Drill-down on Charts, introduces you to the concept of drill-down in charts, which helps you drill down from a macroscopic view to a more detailed one.

Chapter 5, Exporting Charts, introduces the capability of FusionCharts Suite to be exported as images and PDF documents for use in e-mails and presentations.

Chapter 6, Integrating with Server-side Scripts, explains how to power FusionCharts using server-side technologies such as ASP.NET, PHP, and Java, and drive them through databases.

Chapter 7, Creating Maps for your Applications, introduces you to the interactive maps present in FusionMaps, a part of the FusionCharts Suite. After downloading and setting up FusionMaps, you will be able to create a simple US map and then add drill-down to go from the US map to individual states.

Chapter 8, Selecting the Right Visualization for your Data, takes a step-by-step approach to selecting the right visualization for business dashboards. You start by understanding your dashboard's audience, identify the metrics they need to see, move on to the kind of analysis the metric will need, and finally come to the chart best suited for the case in question. You will also take a closer look at at specialized charts such as gauges and Gantt charts.

Chapter 9, Increasing the Usability of your Charts, rounds up the experience by introducing simple tips and techniques that can make your charts more usable. From obvious tips such as having descriptive captions, to less obvious ones such as removing excess detail from data, these tips will go a long way in making your dashboards more usable.

What you need for this book

In order to follow and and understand the steps and code mentioned in the book, you will require the following software:

◆ FusionCharts Suite Evaluation version, which can be downloaded from www.fusioncharts.com/download

◆ Any text editor to write your HTML, XML, and JavaScript code

◆ Access to a server, when connecting to server-side scripts

Who this book is for

This book is both for beginners and advanced web developers who need to create interactive charts for their web applications. No previous knowledge of FusionCharts Suite is assumed, and the book takes you from downloading it to creating complete reports and dashboards.

Conventions

In this book, you will find several headings appearing frequently.

To give clear instructions of how to complete a procedure or task, we use:

Time for action – heading

1. Action 1

2. Action 2

3. Action 3

Instructions often need some extra explanation so that they make sense, so they are followed with:

What just happened?

This heading explains the working of tasks or instructions that you have just completed.

You will also find some other learning aids in the book, including:

Pop quiz – heading

These are short multiple choice questions intended to help you test your own understanding.

Have a go hero – heading

These set practical challenges and give you ideas for experimenting with what you have learned.

You will also find a number of styles of text that distinguish between different kinds of information. Here are some examples of these styles, and an explanation of their meaning.

Code words in text are shown as follows: " When you run `Index.html`, you will see a page as the following screenshot".

A block of code is set as follows:

```
<chart caption='Harry&apos;s SuperMart' subcaption='Revenue by
  Year' xAxisName='Year' yAxisName='Amount' numberPrefix='$'>
  <set label='2009' value='1487500' />
  <set label='2010' value='2100600' />
  <set label='2011' value='2445400' />
</chart>
```

When we wish to draw your attention to a particular part of a code block, the relevant lines or items are set in bold:

```html
<html>
  <body>
    <div id="chartContainer">FusionCharts will load here!</div>
    <script type="text/javascript">
      <!--FusionCharts.setCurrentRenderer('javascript');
      var myChart = new FusionCharts("../FusionCharts/
      Column3D.swf", "myChartId", "400", "300", "0", "1" );
      myChart.setXMLUrl("Data.xml");
      myChart.render("chartContainer");// -->
    </script>
  </body>
</html>
```

New terms and **important words** are shown in bold. Words that you see on the screen, in menus or dialog boxes for example, appear in the text like this: "Note how the **Dashboard** has a very clean and non-cluttered look, despite the large data set it represents ".

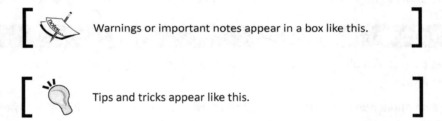

Warnings or important notes appear in a box like this.

Tips and tricks appear like this.

Reader feedback

Feedback from our readers is always welcome. Let us know what you think about this book—what you liked or may have disliked. Reader feedback is important for us to develop titles that you really get the most out of.

To send us general feedback, simply send an e-mail to feedback@packtpub.com, and mention the book title through the subject of your message.

If there is a topic that you have expertise in and you are interested in either writing or contributing to a book, see our author guide on www.packtpub.com/authors.

Customer support

Now that you are the proud owner of a Packt book, we have a number of things to help you to get the most from your purchase.

Downloading the example code

You can download the example code files for all Packt books you have purchased from your account at `http://www.packtpub.com`. If you purchased this book elsewhere, you can visit `http://www.packtpub.com/support` and register to have the files e-mailed directly to you.

Errata

Although we have taken every care to ensure the accuracy of our content, mistakes do happen. If you find a mistake in one of our books—maybe a mistake in the text or the code—we would be grateful if you would report this to us. By doing so, you can save other readers from frustration and help us improve subsequent versions of this book. If you find any errata, please report them by visiting `http://www.packtpub.com/support`, selecting your book, clicking on the **errata submission form** link, and entering the details of your errata. Once your errata are verified, your submission will be accepted and the errata will be uploaded to our website, or added to any list of existing errata, under the Errata section of that title.

Piracy

Piracy of copyright material on the Internet is an ongoing problem across all media. At Packt, we take the protection of our copyright and licenses very seriously. If you come across any illegal copies of our works, in any form, on the Internet, please provide us with the location address or website name immediately so that we can pursue a remedy.

Please contact us at `copyright@packtpub.com` with a link to the suspected pirated material.

We appreciate your help in protecting our authors, and our ability to bring you valuable content.

Questions

You can contact us at `questions@packtpub.com` if you are having a problem with any aspect of the book, and we will do our best to address it.

1
Introducing FusionCharts

As web developers, we build applications that feed on data. We parse it, process it and report it. Our reports take the form of tables, grids, and diagrams such as charts, gauges, and maps. Parsing and processing are backend tasks that are unseen by the user. The actual reporting of data, however, is the bulk of the experience a user has with our application.

To make our reports interesting and insightful, it is important to provide a highly engaging and functional face to the data in context. While tables, grids, and basic charting are natively supported by most web scripting languages, creating advanced or interactive charts require the use of third-party components. FusionCharts Suite is one such suite of components that help you deliver a delightful experience by aiding the creation of animated and interactive charts, gauges, and maps.

Before we jump in and look at what FusionCharts can do for you, let us see where charts, gauges, and maps can be helpful. Google Analytics, a tool that most web developers swear by, is a beautiful example of effective data presentation. In case you do not know, it is a tool that records a ton of information such as visitor demographics, referrers, advertising, browser information, and so on. With so much data recorded, it is of utmost importance to present it in a compact, yet insightful way, as shown in the following screenshot:

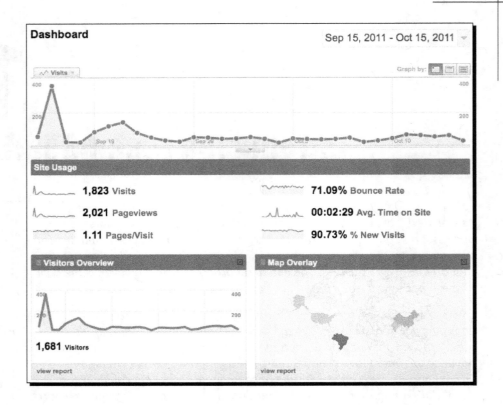

Note how the Dashboard has a very clean and non-cluttered look, despite the large data set it represents. Extra information, which is not required in the main layout, is displayed as tool tips and annotations. Interactive features such as a clickable world map lets you explore the data the way you want to. The selection of chart types is also immaculate, with the line chart showing the trend of the most commonly used metric—the number of visitors to the site. Other relevant metrics such as Pageviews and Pages/Visit are communicated in large text along with sparklines providing a historical context. A world map is used to display where the traffic is coming from.

FusionCharts Suite helps you build similar dashboards with a lot more chart types and interactivity. Without further ado, let us proceed and set the goals for this chapter.

In this chapter, you will:

- Learn how to set up FusionCharts

- Build your first chart and configure basic parameters

- Understand the **eXtensible Markup Language** (**XML**) and **JavaScript Object Notation** (**JSON**) data format supported by FusionCharts and different ways to provide it to the chart

- Learn how to build charts with multiple series and axes

- Create advanced charts such as **Combination charts**

What is FusionCharts Suite?

FusionCharts Suite is a collection of four products, each of which help generate different types of charts, gauges, or maps in web applications. These data-visualization components are ideal for use within reports, dashboards, analytics, surveys, and monitors in web and enterprise applications. The visualizations are rendered using both Adobe Flash and JavaScript (HTML5), thereby making the experience seamless across PCs, Macs and a wide spectrum of devices including iPads and iPhones.

The four products in the suite are:

- **FusionCharts XT**: This helps create the 45 most used chart types such as pie, column, bar, area, line, stacked, combination, and advanced ones such as Pareto and Marimekko.

- **FusionWidgets XT**: This helps create **Key Performance Indicators** (**KPI**) and make real-time data in dashboards, monitors, and reports more insightful. It includes a wide variety of charts and gauges such as dial charts, linear gauges, Gantt charts, funnel charts, sparklines, data-streaming column, line, and area charts.

- **PowerCharts XT**: This helps create charts for domain-specific usage such as those in network diagrams, performance analysis, profit-loss analysis, financial planning, stock price plotting, and hierarchical structures.

- **FusionMaps XT**: This consists of over 550 geographical maps, including all countries, US states, and regions in Europe for plotting business data.

All the products are built on a common framework and offer similar ways to use and configure them. To start with, we will create charts using FusionCharts XT and later explore charts of other products in *Chapter 8, Selecting the Right Visualization for your Data* and *Chapter 7, Creating Maps for your Applications*. Without further ado, let us get started and build our first chart. For that, you will first need to download FusionCharts Suite.

Getting FusionCharts

FusionCharts allows you to download the trial version from its website `http://www.fusioncharts.com`. This trial does not have any feature restriction or an expiry date. The only caveat is that the charts in the evaluation version have *FusionCharts* printed on the chart, which can be removed by purchasing a license of FusionCharts and later just replacing the **Shockwave (SWF)** and **JavaScript (JS)** files, as we shall see later.

Time for action – downloading and extracting FusionCharts

1. Go to `http://www.fusioncharts.com/download` and fill in your particulars in the download form and click on **Download**.

2. On the next page, you will find links to either download the entire FusionCharts Suite, or individual products from the suite. In this chapter, we will work with FusionCharts XT only and hence will explore that.

3. Once the ZIP file has been downloaded, extract it to a folder on your hard drive, which is conveniently located at `C:\FusionChartsSuite\FusionChartsXT` on Windows or `Users/{YourName}/FusionChartsSuite/FusionChartsXT` on Mac or UNIX based systems. Throughout this book, we will refer to this folder as the **FusionCharts Installation Folder**.

 The steps to install and use FusionCharts remain the same, whether you are using the trial or licensed version.

What just happened?

You have now successfully downloaded FusionCharts XT and extracted it in the FusionCharts Installation Folder. We will soon learn how to use these files to build charts. Before that, let us quickly explore the contents of the FusionCharts package.

Within the FusionCharts Installation Folder, you will find multiple folders. Some of the folders are internal folders used to store documentation and gallery files, for example, `Contents`, `Gallery`, and so on. The folders that you will mostly use are `Charts`, `Code`, `SourceCode`, `ExportHandlers`, and the `Tools` folder for the following purpose:

Folder Name	What it contains?
Charts	Contains all the SWF and JS files that form the core of FusionCharts – we will refer to it as **Core FusionCharts** files. The FusionCharts SWF files have been created using Adobe Flash 8 and need Flash Player 8 (or above) to run. The JavaScript is compatible with IE6 (or above), Firefox, Chrome, Opera, and Safari, including that on iPads and iPhones.
Code	Consists of code samples in various programming languages that you can explore, to quickly learn or get started with.
SourceCode	Present only with the Enterprise and Enterprise Plus license, this folder contains the source code of FusionCharts in both Flash Source files (.fla) and JavaScript files.
Tools	Consists of utility applications in three subfolders: FCDataConverter helps you convert the FusionCharts XML data to JSON data and vice versa. We will explore this later in the chapter, after we have created our first chart. FlashPlayerSecuritySetup contains scripts that help you configure security settings on your local machine only when using FusionCharts with JavaScript. We will explore this later in the book when we build advanced examples of FusionCharts integrated with JavaScript. XMLGenerator is a visual interface to generate XML data for FusionCharts. This is primarily intended for non developers and would not be of much help to us.

The FusionCharts Installation Folder also contains three files in the root folder:

Filename	What it contains?
FusionCharts License Agreement.rtf	Contains the license agreement that governs the usage of FusionCharts. You may want to read through it before using FusionCharts.
Version.txt	Contains the detailed version history of FusionCharts XT.
Index.html	The main page that you use to start exploring the FusionCharts package.

When you run `Index.html`, you will see a page similar to the following screenshot:

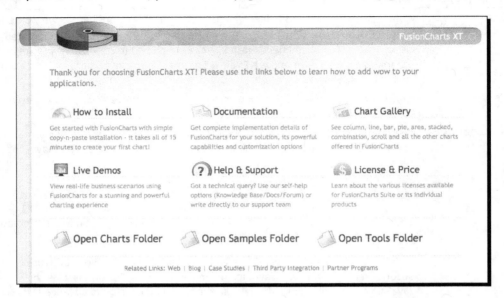

When you click on the **Documentation** link, it opens the documentation for FusionCharts XT, as shown in the following screenshot:

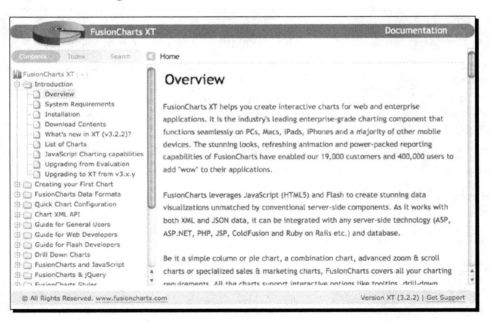

This documentation is an exhaustive resource for FusionCharts including sections for beginners, chart parameter lists, API references, and sections on advanced charting. In this book, we will not repeat, but rather refer to the APIs and parameters explained in the documentation.

From `Index.html`, you can also explore all the chart types present in FusionCharts XT by clicking on **Chart Gallery**. It presents a list of chart types and multiple examples for each, as shown in the following screenshot. We recommend you spend some time exploring this, as this is a good learning resource to get a real-world feel of the charts and understand what you can create once you are familiar with FusionCharts.

The **Live Demos** section, accessible from `Index.html`, lets you explore sample dashboards and examples created using FusionCharts—both offline and online.

Now that you have had a taste of what FusionCharts can do for you, it is time to create your own chart, your first chart using FusionCharts.

Creating your first chart

In our examples, we will create charts for a fictional supermarket, Harry's SuperMart, so that Harry, the owner of the supermarket, can make more sense out of his data. Harry's SuperMart, with 11 stores located in four states in the US, offering over 2,000 types of products and a customer base of around 25,000, records an intensive amount of data, which when presented effectively gives a lot of actionable insights. We will learn how to build meaningful charts that can facilitate this. For our first chart, let us build a simple **Revenue by Year** chart.

Once completed, the chart should look similar to the following screenshot:

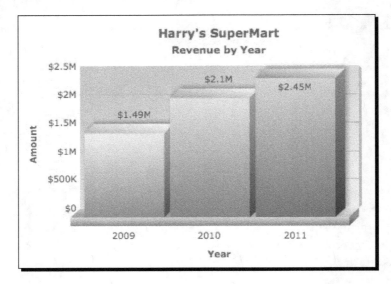

Steps to create a chart using FusionCharts

Fundamentally, for each chart you build, you should ask yourself the following questions to ensure that the chart serves a meaningful purpose, as opposed to just being a fancy object on the page:

◆ Who will view this chart and why will this data interest him? This person is the end user.

◆ What type of chart is best suited to represent this data? Are there any alternate charts that we can use?

◆ Is this chart part of a bigger report/dashboard, or standalone? This helps us decide how to split information across multiple charts.

For our first chart that we build, Harry is the end user. This chart lets him compare the revenues of this year against the last two years. We would plot this data on a 3D Column chart, as Harry uses this to compare the revenues instead of seeing the overall trend. Had Harry wanted to see the trend of revenues over multiple years, we would have used an area or line chart. Also, to keep things simple, we will build this as a standalone chart.

Thereafter, technically, there are three steps to build a chart using FusionCharts:

1. Set up FusionCharts for the entire application, typically done only once per application.
2. Encode the data for the chart, either in XML or JSON format.
3. Write the HTML and JavaScript code to include the chart in a web page.

Let us cover them one-by-one.

Time for action – set up FusionCharts for our first chart

1. Create a folder on your hard-drive to centrally store all the examples that we will build iteratively. If you are working on a web server, you can create this under the root folder of the web application. Let us name it as LearningFusionCharts. You can give it any other name as well.

Downloading the example code

You can download the example code files for all Packt books you have purchased from your account at http://www.packtpub.com. If you purchased this book elsewhere, you can visit http://www.packtpub.com/support and register to have the files e-mailed directly to you.

2. Create a subfolder called FusionCharts within this folder. This folder will contain all the SWF and JavaScript files of FusionCharts, which are the **FusionCharts Core** files. If you are working on a web server, create this folder under the root of the web application, so that the entire web application can conveniently access this.

3. Copy all the SWF and JS files from the Charts folder under the FusionCharts Installation Folder (where you had earlier downloaded and extracted the FusionCharts ZIP file) to the newly created FusionCharts folder. This step completes the installation of FusionCharts for your application.

4. Create another folder under LearningFusionCharts and name it as FirstChart. This will be used to store the XML data and the HTML file for our first chart.

Upgrading the FusionCharts version, or converting from trial to licensed

If you are upgrading to a newer version of FusionCharts, or converting from evaluation to a licensed version, all you need to do is copy the SWF and JS files from the new or licensed version and overwrite the existing files in the FusionCharts folder.

What just happened?

You just installed FusionCharts. It involved copying of all the SWF and JavaScript files of FusionCharts, which are the FusionCharts Core files. If you intend to plot just a subset of chart types, you can select only those SWF files and paste them here. However, copying all files makes it easier in the future whenever you need to create a new chart type in your application. Each SWF file is used to plot a particular type of chart in Flash and the name of the file represents the chart type. You can find the complete list of charts in **FusionCharts Documentation | Introduction | List of Charts**. For our first chart, we are going to use Column3D.swf to plot a 3D Column chart.

The FusionCharts folder also contains six JavaScript files that aid in embedding and configuring charts, along with rendering them in JavaScript when viewed on devices that do not support Flash. These files are as follows:

Filename of the JavaScript Class	Purpose
FusionCharts.js	This is the main JavaScript class for FusionCharts, which helps you embed charts in your web pages in a user-friendly way, and offers functionalities such as updating chart data, retrieving chart data, supporting multiple data formats, and event handling.
FusionCharts.HC.js	This framework contains code to render FusionCharts in JavaScript.
FusionCharts.HC.Charts.js	Contains chart specific code to render FusionCharts XT in JavaScript.
jquery.min.js	Minified jQuery framework used by FusionCharts class for internal functions.
FusionCharts.jqueryplugin.js	FusionCharts jQuery class that lets you embed FusionCharts using jQuery syntax.
FusionChartsExportComponent.js	The charts generated by FusionCharts can be exported as images or PDFs in the browser itself, using a module called Client-side Export Component, as we will see later. This JavaScript file provides interfaces to link the Client-side Export Component to the charts.

While creating your chart, as you will soon see, you just need to include `FusionCharts.js` in your page. The other files such as `FusionCharts.HC.js`, `FusionCharts.HC.Charts.js`, and `jquery.min.js` are dynamically loaded by the code in `FusionCharts.js`.

With the basic setup in place, let us focus on the data for our chart.

Time for action – creating XML data for our first chart

1. Create an empty XML file within the `FirstChart` folder named as `Data.xml`. This can be done using your text editor (Notepad on Windows, or TextEdit on Mac). To do so, while saving an empty text file, rename the extension to `.xml`.

2. Write the following XML code in the file and save it:

```
<chart caption='Harry&apos;s SuperMart' subcaption='Revenue by
  Year' xAxisName='Year' yAxisName='Amount' numberPrefix='$'>
  <set label='2009' value='1487500' />
  <set label='2010' value='2100600' />
  <set label='2011' value='2445400' />
</chart>
```

3. Check whether the XML is valid by opening `Data.xml` in Internet Explorer or Firefox. If the browser shows the XML properly, you are good to go. Otherwise, review the error message and fix the error in XML accordingly.

What just happened?

Here, we have encoded the data, as shown in the following table, to an XML format supported by FusionCharts:

Year	Revenue
2009	$1,487,500
2010	$2,100,600
2011	$2,445,400

Each chart in FusionCharts is powered by data. This data could be static and hand-coded as we will build in this example, or dynamically generated by live scripts that are connected to databases or web services which we will explore later in *Chapter 6, Integrating with Server-side Scripts*. FusionCharts can accept this data in two formats—XML and JSON. Both are commonly used formats for data exchange on the Web, with XML being easy on the human eyes.

The XML format that we just created is called single-series XML in FusionCharts parlance, as we are plotting just one series of data. Later in this chapter, we will explore multi-series charts that let you compare more than one series of data, for example, revenue split across Food and Non-Food products for each year across last three years.

All FusionCharts XML files start with the `<chart>` element. The attributes of the `<chart>` element help you configure the functional and cosmetic properties of the chart. In our example, we have defined the chart caption, subcaption, axis titles, and the currency prefix for numbers on the chart, as in the following line of code:

```
<chart caption='Harry&apos;s SuperMart' subcaption='Revenue by Year'
    xAxisName='Year' yAxisName='Amount' numberPrefix='$'>
```

For each chart type, there are hundreds of optional attributes that you can define. If these are not defined, the chart assumes the default values for each of them.

Special characters in XML need to be encoded

XML documents can contain non-ASCII characters or special characters. However, these need to be encoded before they are provided in the XML document. In our example, note how we have encoded the apostrophe in Harry's to `Harry&apos;s`. Had we not done that, the XML document would have been an invalid one and raised errors when opened in a browser.

Each row of data to be plotted on the chart is represented by the `<set>` element. The `label` attribute defines the text label for each data point, and the `value` attribute defines its numerical value to be plotted. There are additional attributes that can be defined for the `<set>` element, for example, user-defined colors, which we will explore in later chapters. An important thing to note is how the $ prefix or comma separators have been stripped off the revenue numbers, before encoding them as a value for the `<set>` element, that is, $1,487,500 has been converted to 1487500, as shown in the following line of code:

```
<set … value='1487500' />
```

This is necessary as FusionCharts can interpret only standard numeric values.

While the standard attributes for the `<chart>` and `<set>` elements are common across chart types, many chart types have special features that are controlled by attributes that are specific for the chart. You can explore a list of all such attributes for each chart in the documentation of FusionCharts, under the section **Chart XML API**.

With both the basic setup and data in place, we are just one step away from seeing our chart live—writing the HTML and JavaScript to embed this chart, which we will do next.

Time for action – Writing the HTML and JavaScript code to embed the chart

1. Create an empty HTML file within the `FirstChart` folder named as `FirstChart.html`.

2. Paste the following code in the file and save it:

```
<html>
  <head>
    <title>My First chart using FusionCharts</title>
    <script type="text/javascript"
      src="../FusionCharts/FusionCharts.js">
    </script>
  </head>
  <body>
    <div id="chartContainer">FusionCharts will load here!</div>
    <script type="text/javascript">
    <!-- var myChart =
      new FusionCharts("../FusionCharts/Column3D.swf",
      "myChartId", "400", "300", "0", "1" );
      myChart.setXMLUrl("Data.xml");
      myChart.render("chartContainer");//-->
    </script>
  </body>
</html>
```

3. Open it in a web browser. You should see your first chart coming to life, as shown in the following screenshot. Refresh the browser to experience the animation again, or hover over the columns to see tooltips.

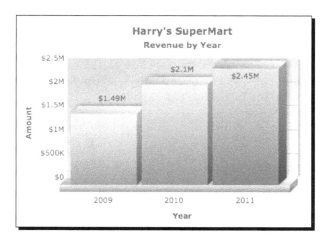

4. If you have access to an iPad or iPhone, open this example using the device. To do so, upload the entire `LearningFusionCharts` to a server that can be accessed over the Internet. Now point the browser in the device to `http://Your_Website_URL/FirstChart/FirstChart.html`. You will be able to see the same chart, but this time, rendered using JavaScript. The following screenshot shows a rendering of the chart within Safari in an iPhone. Tap on the columns to see the tool-tips.

What just happened?

You just created your first chart, that's what happened! This chart renders using Adobe Flash on devices that support it, and automatically switches to JavaScript rendering on devices such as iPads and iPhones. The beauty of the solution is that no additional code or configuration is required to do this.

Let us break down our HTML and JavaScript code into digestible chunks. To create charts using FusionCharts in your page, you first need to include the FusionCharts JavaScript library (`FusionCharts.js`), as in the following lines of code:

```
<script type="text/javascript" src="../FusionCharts/FusionCharts.js">
  </script>
```

Note that you only need to include `FusionCharts.js` in your code. The other files required for FusionCharts, namely `FusionCharts.HC.js`, `FusionCharts.HC.Charts.js`, and `jquery.min.js` are dynamically loaded by code in `FusionCharts.js`.

Next, we create a DIV as a placeholder where the chart would be rendered. We give the DIV an ID—chartContainer. This is done using the following code:

```
<div id="chartContainer">FusionCharts will load here!</div>
```

The DIV carries a placeholder text FusionCharts will load here! which will be displayed if there is an error in your JavaScript code, or FusionCharts.js or the chart SWF file could not be loaded. If you see this text instead of the chart, you know what to fix.

Following this, we initialize a chart by invoking the FusionCharts JavaScript constructor, using the following code:

```
var myChart = new FusionCharts("../FusionCharts/Column3D.swf",
  "myChartId", "400", "300", "0", "1" );
```

To this constructor, we pass the following parameters in order:

1. **Path and filename of the chart SWF**: The first parameter contains the path and filename of the chart SWF file. We have used the relative path to the SWF file, which is recommended.

2. **ID of the chart**: Each chart on the page needs a unique ID. This ID is different from the ID of the container DIV. As we will learn later, this ID is used to get a reference of the chart for manipulation using advanced JavaScript.

3. **Width and height in pixels**: Each chart needs to be initialized with width and height, specified either in pixels (specified in numeric format, without appending px) or percentage. In this example, we have used pixels. You can also set it to % values as in the following code:

```
var myChart = new FusionCharts("../FusionCharts/Column3D.swf",
  "myChartId", "100%", "100%", "0", "1" );
```

The FusionCharts JavaScript class will automatically convert the % dimensions to pixel dimensions, with respect to the parent container element in HTML, DIV in this case, and pass it to the chart.

4. **Whether to start the chart in Debug mode**: While developing your charts, if you face any issues, you can initialize them in debug mode by setting this parameter to 1. The Debug mode gives you behind-the-scenes information on where the data is loaded from, errors, and so on. In our example, we are rendering the chart in normal mode, by setting this parameter to 0.

5. In previous versions of FusionCharts, you had to manually set the last parameter to 1, if you wanted FusionCharts to communicate with JavaScript. Now that FusionCharts is very well integrated with JavaScript, this parameter is a mandatory 1.

Alternate compact constructor method

A chart can also be initialized using the `static render()` method of the FusionCharts class, as shown below.

```
<script type="text/javascript">
  <!--var myChart = FusionCharts.render
  ("../FusionCharts/Column3D.swf", "myChartId",
    "400", "300",
  "chartContainer", "Data.xml"); // -->
</script>
```

There are additional possible syntaxes of this constructor and are detailed in **FusionCharts Documentation | FusionCharts and JavaScript | Constructor methods**.

Once the chart is constructed, we tell the chart where to source data from. We use a relative path to `Data.xml`, as it is stored in the same folder.

```
myChart.setXMLUrl("Data.xml");
```

If you recall, FusionCharts accepts data in two formats – XML and JSON – either provided as a string or a URL that points to the data file. In our example, we have used XML as the data format, which is stored in `Data.xml`. So, we use the `setXMLURL()` function to pass the URL of the XML data file to the chart.

What if the XML data file was stored in another location or subdomain?

If your data file was stored in a different folder, you would have to specify the relative path to the folder and then the filename, for example, `../ Source/Data/MyData.xml`. We do not recommend specifying absolute URLs, because, if you move your web page or data file to another domain, cross-domain security issues would crop up and the chart would stop working.

Flash Player's sandbox security model blocks loading of files across different sub-domains. If you need to load your XML data from another subdomain, you will have to create a Cross domain policy XML file, as explained at `http://www.adobe.com/devnet/articles/crossdomain_ policy_file_spec.html`.

Finally, to render the chart in the `DIV` that you had earlier created, you invoke the `render()` function and pass to it the ID of the `DIV`.

```
myChart.render("chartContainer");
```

Do remember that each chart and DIV needs to have its own unique ID.

What to look for if your chart is not rendered?

If you do not see any chart, there could be multiple reasons behind it. You should check for the following, based on what you see in your browser:

What do you currently see instead of the chart?	Corrective measures you should take
"FusionCharts will load here!" text that you had placed in the container DIV	Check whether the `FusionCharts` folder is present in the `LearningFusionCharts` folder and contains all JavaScript files required for FusionCharts.
	Check whether you have provided the correct relative path to `FusionCharts.js` in the page `FirstChart.html`.
	Check for errors in your JavaScript code that you have written to embed the chart. Use the browser's developer tools to check this.
	Ensure that you have given different IDs for container `DIV`, chart JavaScript variable and the chart object in the constructor.
Empty white area instead of the chart	Check whether you have copied `Column3D.swf` to the `FusionCharts` folder.
	Check whether the relative path provided to `Column3D.swf` in FusionCharts constructor is correct.
"Error in loading data"	Check whether `Data.xml` is present within the `FirstChart` folder
	Check whether the path specified to `Data.xml` is correct in the `setXMLUrl()` method.
"Invalid data"	Check for the validity of XML data in `Data.xml` by opening it in a browser or an XML editor. Or, you can also switch the debug mode of chart to ON by changing the last but one parameter in constructor to `1`. That will highlight the error in XML, as shown in the following screenshot:

With these measures, you should be able to locate the error and get your chart working. Before we move ahead to explore the other aspects of FusionCharts, let us understand how FusionCharts automatically switches between Flash and JavaScript mode.

Converting the chart to a pure JavaScript chart

By default, FusionCharts renders its charts using Adobe Flash. However, as you have seen earlier, when you view the chart on iPads or iPhones, FusionCharts automatically switches to JavaScript rendering, as Flash is not supported on those devices. This is internally checked by `FusionCharts.js`, and the auto-loaded files `FusionCharts.HC.js`, `FusionCharts.HC.Charts.js`, and `jquery.min.js` then aid in rendering the chart using JavaScript, using the same datasource and configuration.

FusionCharts also provides an option to entirely skip Flash rendering and use JavaScript as the default rendering, irrespective of the device. This feature can be very nifty for developers who want to develop JavaScript-only applications or even frameworks. Let us quickly see how to attain that.

Time for action – creating JavaScript only charts

1. Create a copy of our `FirstChart.html` in the same location and name it as `JavaScriptChart.html`.

2. Add the following lines of code, as highlighted, before the constructor.

```
<html>
  <body>
    <div id="chartContainer">FusionCharts will load here!</div>
    <script type="text/javascript">
      <!--FusionCharts.setCurrentRenderer('javascript');
        var myChart =
        new FusionCharts("../FusionCharts/Column3D.swf",
        "myChartId", "400", "300", "0", "1" );
      myChart.setXMLUrl("Data.xml");
      myChart.render("chartContainer");// -->
    </script>
  </body>
</html>
```

3. Open the page in a browser. You should see the same chart as earlier, but this time rendered using JavaScript. It has animations and interactivity similar to the Flash version as shown in the following screenshot:

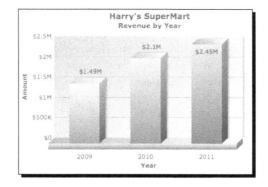

How different is the Flash rendering from JavaScript rendering?

The JavaScript version of FusionCharts behaves similar to the Flash version, offering most of the functional and cosmetic configuration. With the exception of a true 3D chart, all charts look and behave almost the same as their Flash counterpart. There are minor visual differences in the JavaScript version such as the width of columns, effect of shadows, handling of long x-axis labels, appearance of scroll bars, and so on. A detailed list of such differences are present in **FusionCharts Documentation | Introduction | JavaScript Charting Capabilities | How different is JavaScript charts from Flash charts?**

What just happened?

You just converted the previous chart to a pure JavaScript chart, irrespective of the device it is now viewed on. The following snippet of code instructs FusionCharts to switch the rendering mode to JavaScript:

```
FusionCharts.setCurrentRenderer('javascript');
```

If your page contains multiple charts, this setting applies to all such charts that are defined after this line of code. Hence, if you declare this at the beginning, all the charts in the page will render using JavaScript. You would not need to declare the same for each chart in the page.

JavaScript cannot access data stored on your hard drive in some browsers

Some browsers restrict JavaScript from accessing the local filesystem due to security reasons. Hence, the JavaScript charts, when running from your local hard drive, would not be able to access XML or JSON data provided as a URL. However, when run from a server, including localhost, they will run fine. An alternate method to get JavaScript charts working locally is to use the Data String method, which we will explore in the next section.

Have a go hero – build a dashboard for Harry

In this example, you created a standalone Column 3D chart. How about inching towards building a complete dashboard? To do so, convert the existing chart to a Column 2D chart and add the following three charts to this page. In addition, specify different width and height for each chart to accommodate the amount of data it presents, and also place them in order of importance of the chart to Harry.

- A Line 2D chart, using `Line.swf`, comparing monthly revenues for this year. For this, you need to create an XML data with the `<set>` element for each month of the year.

- A Pie 2D chart, using `Pie2D.swf`, showing the composition of expenses of this year split under these categories: Salary, Cost of Goods, Marketing Costs, Overheads, and Administration.

- A Column 2D chart, using `Column2D.swf`, showing the top five salespersons for the year.

All these charts use the same single-series XML format that you had earlier created. Remember to provide a different ID for each chart and its container `DIV`. Also, do not forget to encode special characters such as `&` (ampersand) or `'` (apostrophe) in XML.

Once you are done, let us explore the other way to provide XML data to FusionCharts—as a string, instead of providing a URL, for example, `Data.xml`.

Using the Data String method to provide data

As we had mentioned earlier, there are two ways to provide data to FusionCharts – either as a URL to the datasource (**Data URL method**), or as a string (**Data String method**). Till now, we have used the former method by invoking the `setXMLUrl()` method on the chart instance and providing `Data.xml` as the URL. In order to pass the XML as a string to the chart, we can use the `setXMLData()` method, as explained next.

Time for action – embedding XML in the web page and using the Data String method

1. Create a copy of our `FirstChart.html` in the same location and name it as `DataStringMethod.html`.

2. Change the following lines in code, as highlighted:

```
<html>
  <body>
    <div id="chartContainer">FusionCharts will load here!</div>
```

```
<script type="text/javascript">
  <!-- var myChart =
    new FusionCharts("../FusionCharts/Column3D.swf",
    "myChartId", "400","300", "0", "1" );
    myChart.setXMLData("<chart
      caption='Harry&apos;s SuperMart'
      subcaption='Revenue by Year' xAxisName='Year'
      yAxisName='Amount' numberPrefix='$'>\
    <set label='2009' value='1487500' />\
    <set label='2010' value='2100600' />\
    <set label='2011' value='2445400' />\
    </chart>");
    myChart.render("chartContainer");// -->
  </script>
 </body>
</html>
```

3.   Open the page in a browser. You should see the same chart as earlier, but this time using data embedded in the page, and not `Data.xml`.

What just happened?

You just used the Data String method of FusionCharts to power up your chart using XML data embedded in the page, instead of reading it from `Data.xml`. This was done by invoking the `setXMLData()` method on the chart instance.

```
myChart.setXMLData("<chart caption='Harry&apos;s SuperMart'
  subcaption='Revenue by Year' xAxisName='Year' yAxisName='Amount'
  numberPrefix='$'>\
  <set label='2009' value='1487500' />\
  <set label='2010' value='2100600' />\
  <set label='2011' value='2445400' />\
  </chart>");
```

The entire XML string is passed to this method. Note how we are using the \ characters in JavaScript to split the XML data string into multiple lines for enhanced readability. Make sure there are no trailing spaces, when using this approach.

You can also define a JavaScript string variable, store XML data in it, and then assign the variable reference to the chart instance, as shown in the following code snippet:

```
<html>
  <body>
    <div id="chartContainer">FusionCharts will load here!</div>
    <script type="text/javascript"><!-- var strData =
      "<chart caption='Harry&apos;s SuperMart' subcaption='Revenue by
      Year' xAxisName='Year' yAxisName='Amount' numberPrefix='$'>" +
```

```
        "<set label='2009' value='1487500' />" +
        "<set label='2010' value='2100600' />" +
        "<set label='2011' value='2445400' />" + "</chart>";
        var myChart = new FusionCharts("../FusionCharts/Column3D.swf",
        "myChartId", "400", "300", "0", "1" );
        myChart.setXMLData(strData);
        myChart.render("chartContainer");// -->
    </script>
  </body>
</html>
```

In the previous example, we had stored the entire XML string in the variable `strData`, and then passed its reference to the `setXMLData()` method, instead of the XML string directly.

When using this method to provide data, if your chart is not working or reporting `Invalid data`, check for the following:

- ◆ Make sure that the quotation marks specified in JavaScript to provide parameters and in XML to provide attributes are different. Otherwise, it will result in a JavaScript syntax error. To keep things easy to remember, use double quotation marks for JavaScript, and single quotation marks for XML attributes.

- ◆ Ensure that special characters such as ', ", &, <, and > present as XML attribute values are encoded to `&apos;`, `&quot;`, `&amp;`, `&lt;`, and `&gt;` respectively.

Now that you are familiar with both the ways of providing XML data to FusionCharts, let us explore the other data format supported by FusionCharts—JSON.

Using JSON data with FusionCharts

JSON is a lightweight and simple data format derived from JavaScript. The data structure is language-independent, with encoders and parsers available for virtually every programming language. FusionCharts allows you to provide JSON data to the chart either as a URL using the `setJSONUrl()` method or as a string using the `setJSONData()` method. Before we use these methods, let us convert our previous data from XML format to JSON format to understand this format. To do this, we will use the **FusionCharts Data Format Conversion Tool** that comes in the FusionCharts download package. Perform the following steps:

Time for action – converting FusionCharts XML format to JSON

1. Launch the `FCDataConverter` tool from the FusionCharts Installation Folder | `Tools` | `FCDataConverter` | `Index.html`.

2. Once the page has finished loading, in the text area on the left, titled **FusionCharts XML Data**, paste the XML data that we had previously created for **Revenue by Year** chart.

3. Click on the **Convert to JSON** button present below it.

4. In the text area on the right, you will now see the JSON equivalent of the XML data, as shown in the following screenshot:

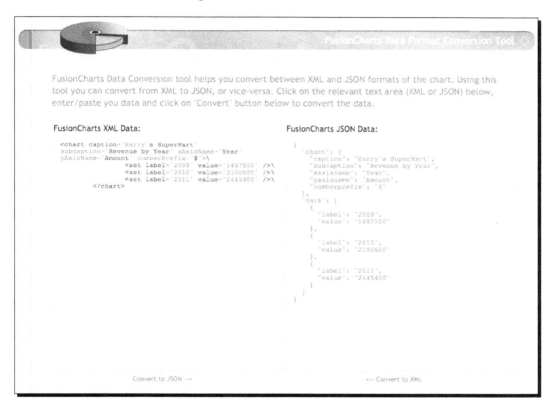

What just happened?

Using the FusionCharts Data Format Conversion Tool, you just converted the previous XML data into JSON format. It reads as in the following code snippet:

```
{
  "chart": {
    "caption": "Harry's SuperMart",
    "subcaption": "Revenue by Year",
    "xaxisname": "Year",
    "yaxisname": "Amount",
```

```
      "numberprefix": "$"
    },
    "data": [
      {
        "label": "2009",
        "value": "1487500"
      },
      {
        "label": "2010",
        "value": "2100600"
      },
      {
        "label": "2011",
        "value": "2445400"
      }
    ]
  }
```

Similar to XML, the `chart` object contains attributes that let you configure functional and cosmetic aspects of the chart.

In the most general form, chart attributes represent the following JSON format:

```
"attributeName" : "Value"
```

For example, `"xAxisName" : "Year"`

The attributes can occur in any order and values can be specified either using double quotes or single, for example, `xAxisName:'Year'`. However, you need to ensure that the same attribute is not defined twice for any element, as it results in an invalid XML.

Escaping of special characters is not compulsory in the JSON URL format

When using the JSON data format, special characters are not encoded to XML entities. Instead, they are escaped in JavaScript using \. However, this is not mandatory when using JSON URL as data, as JavaScript loads the JSON data and directly parses attributes as string literals. Hence, in our example, Harry's SuperMart does not need to be encoded as we had done in the XML format.

However, if you have a mismatch of JavaScript enclosing quotes and JSON attribute quotes, as we will see in our next example, escaping is required.

Next, the array `data` contains all the data points to be plotted on the chart. For example, in XML, `label` attribute for each data point defines its text label, and the `value` attribute represents its numerical value. Each element in the `data` array is an unnamed object defined in the following format:

```
{ "label: "Jan", "value" : "17400", "otherAttribute" : "value"}
```

With the JSON format understood, let us also look at how to use the `setJSONUrl()` and `setJSONData()` methods.

Time for action – powering a chart using JSON data stored in a file

1. Create a file `Data.json` in the `FirstChart` folder.

2. Paste the previously converted JSON in this file and save it.

3. Create a copy of `FirstChart.html` in the same folder and name it as `JSONDataURL.html`.

4. Change the following lines of code, as highlighted:

```html
<html>
  <body>
    <div id="chartContainer">FusionCharts will load here!</div>
    <script type="text/javascript"><!-- var myChart =
      new FusionCharts("../FusionCharts/Column3D.swf",
      "myChartId","400", "300", "0", "1" );
      myChart.setJSONUrl("Data.json");
      myChart.render("chartContainer");// -->
    </script>
  </body>
</html>
```

5. View the page in the browser. You should see the same chart as the previous one.

What just happened?

You just configured your chart to use JSON data as URL, instead of XML. If you do not see a chart, however, your browser might be restricting JavaScript to load local files. In that case, you will have to switch to the JSON Data String method, as explained in the next section.

Time for action – powering a chart using JSON data embedded in the page

1. Create a copy of `DataStringMethod.html` in the `FirstChart` folder and name it as `DataStringMethodJSON.html`.

2. Change the following lines of code, as highlighted:

```html
<html>
  <body>
    <div id="chartContainer">FusionCharts will load here!</div>
    <script type="text/javascript">
      <!--var myChart =
      new FusionCharts("../FusionCharts/Column3D.swf",
      "myChartId","400", "300", "0", "1" );
      myChart.setJSONData('{\"chart": {\
      "caption": "Harry\'s SuperMart",\
      "subcaption": "Revenue by Year",\
      "xaxisname": "Year",\
      "yaxisname": "Amount",\
      "numberprefix": "$"\
      },\"data": [{\
      "label": "2009",\
      "value": "1487500"\
      },{\
      "label": "2010",\
      "value": "2100600"\
      },{\
      "label": "2011",\
      "value": "2445400"\
      }]}');
      myChart.render("chartContainer");// -->
    </script>
  </body>
</html>
```

3. View the page in the browser. You should see the same chart as the previous one.

What just happened?

You changed the `setXMLData()` function to the `setJSONData()` function and provided JSON data instead of XML data. Also, note how the apostrophe in `Harry's SuperMart` was escaped in JavaScript so as to form `Harry\'s SuperMart`. Otherwise, there would have been a conflict of quotes leading to invalid JavaScript syntax.

You can also provide the JSON data to the `setJSONData()` method as an object, instead of a string, as shown in the following code:

```html
<html>
  <body>
    <div id="chartContainer">FusionCharts will load here!</div>
    <script type="text/javascript">
    <!-- var myChart =
      new FusionCharts("../FusionCharts/Column3D.swf",
      "myChartId", "400", "300", "0", "1" );
      myChart.setJSONData({
        "chart": {
          "caption": "Harry\'s SuperMart",
          "subcaption": "Revenue by Year",
          "xaxisname": "Year",
          "yaxisname": "Amount",
          "numberprefix": "$"
        },
        "data": [{
        "label": "2009",
        "value": "1487500"
      },{
          "label": "2010",
          "value": "2100600"
      },{
        "label": "2011",
        "value": "2445400"
      }]});
      myChart.render("chartContainer");// -->
    </script>
  </body>
</html>
```

Here, we have converted the JSON string to a JavaScript object by removing the enclosing string quotation marks and even the \ character that was used for concatenating the string distributed across multiple lines. And that does it all!

Bingo! You are now adept with the basics of FusionCharts. You have learned how to create a FusionCharts, provide XML or JSON data as either URL or string, and even render the chart using pure JavaScript. Now, we are all set to explore additional charts in FusionCharts. First, we will create a chart with more than one series of data, called a multi-series chart in FusionCharts parlance.

Creating charts with multiple series

In our previous example, we had built a Column 3D chart with three columns, each column representing the revenue for a specific year. Now, Harry needs to see how the revenue is split across food products and non-food products, each year. He needs this to monitor growth of both the segments over the years. The data for this example is provided in the following table:

Year	Sales of Food Products	Sales of Non-Food Products
2009	892500	595000
2010	1407400	693200
2011	1565000	880400

The sum of food products and non-food products adds up to the total revenue per year, which we had earlier plotted. The set of data points representing one of these segments, says food-products, is a **data series**, or a **dataset** in FusionCharts XML terminology. We have two data series in our next chart that would be rendered side-by-side, as in the following screenshot:

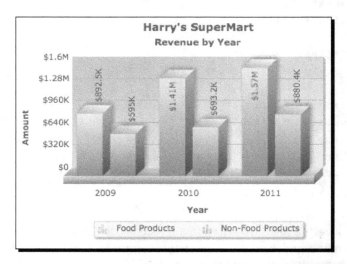

Time for action – creating a multi-series chart

1. Create a copy of FirstChart.html in the FirstChart folder and name it as MultiSeriesChart.html.

2. Change the following lines of code, as highlighted:

```html
<html>
  <body>
    <div id="chartContainer">FusionCharts will load here!</div>
    <script type="text/javascript">
     <!-- var myChart =
        new FusionCharts("../FusionCharts/MSColumn3D.swf",
        "myChartId", "400", "300", "0", "1" );
        myChart.setXMLUrl("MSData.xml");
        myChart.render("chartContainer");// -->
    </script>
  </body>
</html>
```

3. Create a copy of `Data.xml` in the same folder and rename the copy to `MSData.xml`. Write the following XML in this file and save it.

```xml
<chart caption='Harry&apos;s SuperMart' subcaption='Revenue by
Year'
  xAxisName='Year' yAxisName='Amount' numberPrefix='$'
  rotateValues='1'>
  <categories>
    <category label='2009' />
    <category label='2010' />
    <category label='2011' />
  </categories>
  <dataset seriesName='Food Products'>
    <set value='892500' />
    <set value='1407400' />
    <set value='1565000' />
  </dataset>
  <dataset seriesName='Non-Food Products'>
    <set value='595000' />
    <set value='693200' />
    <set value='880400' />
  </dataset>
</chart>
```

4. Open `MultiSeriesChart.html` in your browser. You should now see a chart with two series of columns, as we had planned to build.

What just happened?

In `MultiSeriesChart.html`, we have changed the SWF file from `Column3D.swf` to `MSColumn3D.swf` to render a multi-series chart. FusionCharts uses separate SWF files to plot charts with single series of data (**single-series**) and those with more than one (**multi-series**). Names of SWFs that plot multiple series start with a prefix of `MS`. We have also pointed XML URL to the newly created `MSData.xml`, which contains data in multi-series format for this chart, in the `setXMLUrl()` method. These are the only changes required in the web page.

The bulk of changes are in the XML data file to adapt it to the multi-series format. Let us review them. The multi-series chart XML begins with the `<chart>` element, similar to single-series and all the other charts in FusionCharts. You can provide attributes for the `<chart>` element to configure the functional and cosmetic properties of the chart. In this example, building on top of our earlier single-series chart, we have introduced a new attribute `rotateValues='1'`, that rotates the data values on the chart to accommodate more numbers. The other attributes remain the same.

Next, we have the `<categories>` element that is applicable when you are plotting multi-series charts only. Each child `<category>` element of the `<categories>` element represents an x-axis label (also called the data point's label). The label attribute of the `<category>` element lets you specify them as string values. In our chart, we are comparing the segment-wise sales for 2009, 2010, and 2011, and hence have them as x-axis labels.

```
<categories>
   <category label='2009' />
   <category label='2010' />
   <category label='2011' />
</categories>
```

All that is now left to be defined is data for both the data series. Each series is represented by a `<dataset>` element and attributes of this element lets you specify a custom color for the series, and whether to show or hide data values. To define individual data points within a series, children `<set>` elements are added with a value attribute containing a data point value.

```
<dataset seriesName='Food Products'>
   <set value='892500' />
   <set value='1407400' />
   <set value='1565000' />
</dataset>
```

The data point labels or x-axis labels in `<category>` elements are matched to their respective data point values in the `<set>` element, based on the order of the definition in XML, that is, the first `<category>` element provides the label for the first `<set>` element and so on. To plot a normal chart, the number of `<set>` elements within each `<dataset>` should be equal to the number of defined `<category>` elements.

The previous XML can also be used to plot a stacked chart where columns are placed on top of each other as opposed to side-by-side. The stacked charts are used when the constituents of a data series are relevant along with the sum of all such constituents. While these charts are suited for the comparison of sum, comparison of the constituents against each other is best portrayed by the multi-series chart. To build our stacked chart, we need to change the chart SWF to `StackedColumn3D.swf`. In the XML, we only make a small change to not rotate the data values by removing the `rotateValues='1'` attribute from the `<chart>` element. This results in a chart as shown in the following screenshot:

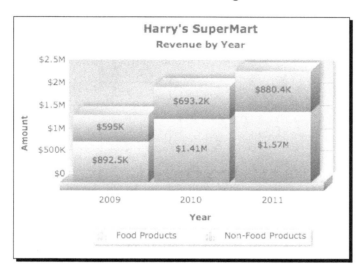

Can multi-series charts be used to plot only one series of data?

Yes, with a few changes. In a single series chart, all the columns are colored differently. In contrast, in a multi-series chart, all the columns of a data series are of the same color, unless explicitly configured not to. Secondly, the multi-series charts show a visual legend indicating the color of each data series. The key in this legend is clickable and lets the end users show or hide the data series.

When plotting a single series of data using a multi-series chart, you need to provide only one `<dataset>` element to contain these data points.

Can the number of <set> and <category> elements mismatch?

No. If you have more `<category>` elements than `<set>` elements in any data series, FusionCharts fails to find data for those additional `<category>` elements and plots an empty space on the chart for the missing data points. In contrast, if the number of `<set>` elements are more than the number of defined `<category>` elements, FusionCharts ignores them, as these data points do not have respective x-axis labels defined for them, and hence would be without context.

In real-life scenarios, you may have missing or non-existent data within a data series. FusionCharts provides a method for you to specify that. Let us consider an example.

Representing missing or non-existent data on the chart

Let us consider a hypothetical example of building this on top of our last example. What if Harry started selling food products only in 2010, when he added refrigeration capabilities? However, non-food products were still sold in 2009. Hence, we would need to tell FusionCharts that data for food products in 2009 is missing or nonexistent. This can be done by specifying an empty `<set/>` element as in the following XML:

```
<chart caption='Harry&apos;s SuperMart' subcaption='Revenue by Year'
  xAxisName='Year' yAxisName='Amount' numberPrefix='$'
  rotateValues='1'>
  <categories>
    <category label='2009' />
    <category label='2010' />
    <category label='2011' />
  </categories>
  <dataset seriesName='Food Products'>
    <set />
    <set value='1407400' />
    <set value='1565000' />
  </dataset>
  <dataset seriesName='Non-Food Products'>
    <set value='595000' />
    <set value='693200' />
    <set value='880400' />
  </dataset>
</chart>
```

This instructs the chart to render an empty space instead of the column representing food-products in 2009, to indicate missing or non-existent data. This method of providing missing data is applicable to all charts in FusionCharts.

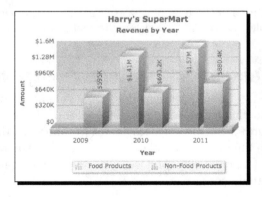

Can missing data be replaced by providing zero values?

You might wonder that if there was no data for 2009, why could we not specify the value as 0. It would mean that Harry's SuperMart was not able to sell any food products in 2009, as opposed to the fact that it did not stock food products then. Both have different meanings and need to be visualized accordingly.

Now that you have an understanding of how to plot multiple series on a chart for comparison, let us consider an extension of multi-series charts—combination charts.

Combination charts

Combination charts let you combine two or more chart types in a single chart, for example, a column chart series and a line chart series. This is done either to highlight specific data series by rendering, or to mix different types of data series on the same chart. There are two types of combination charts possible in FusionCharts.

The first type, called **Single Y-axis combination charts**, have a single y-axis and all the data series conform to it. Some charts in this category are MSCombi2D.swf, MSCombi3D.swf, MSColumnLine3D.swf, and so on. As an example, if you wish to plot the actual revenue versus the projected revenue on a chart, as both the series have the same unit (currency) and magnitude, we plot them against the same axis. However, as the focus is on the actual revenue, it should be plotted using column or area, and the projected revenue can be plotted using lines to show it as guidance.

The second type, called **Dual Y-axes combination charts**, have two y-axes, each having its own units and magnitude. These charts have the abbreviation DY in their name, for example, MSCombiDY2D.swf or MSColumn3DLineDY.swf. Consider a chart where you are plotting the revenue of a company versus the units (quantity) sold. As both the series represent different units, they need to be plotted on different axes. The primary axis can represent the sales, and the second used for units sold. Conventionally, you would represent the sales using columns plotted against the primary axis on the left side of the chart, and the units sold using lines plotting against the secondary axis on the right side of the chart.

Let us build an example of both these charts.

Time for action – the chart showing the actual versus the projected revenue

1. Create a copy of `MultiSeriesChart.html` in the same folder and name it as `ActualVsProjected.html`.

2. Change the reference of the chart SWF file in the embedding code to `MSCombi2D.swf`. This SWF renders a 2D combination chart with a single y-axis.

3. Change the XML URL to `ActualVsProjected.xml` in the chart embedding code.

4. Create an XML file with the name `ActualVsProjected.xml` in the same folder and write the following data in it:

```
<chart caption='Harry&apos;s SuperMart' subcaption='Revenue by
Year'
  xAxisName='Year' yAxisName='Amount' numberPrefix='$'>
  <categories>
    <category label='2009' />
    <category label='2010' />
    <category label='2011' />
  </categories>
  <dataset seriesName='Actual Revenue'>
    <set value='1487500' />
    <set value='2100600' />
    <set value='2445400' />
  </dataset>
  <dataset seriesName='Projected Revenue' renderAs='Line'
    dashed='1' showValues='0' color='666666'>
    <set value='1216500' />
    <set value='2043400' />
    <set value='2292400' />
  </dataset>
</chart>
```

5. Open `ActualVsProjected.html` in your browser. You should see a chart similar to the following screenshot:

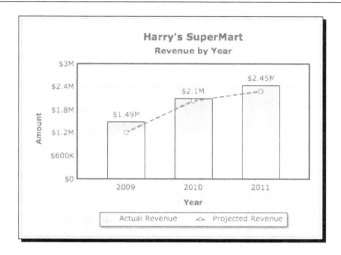

What just happened?

We just created a combination chart to compare the actual revenue of Harry's SuperMart to the projected revenues, which were set as a target. For a change, we have plotted it as a 2D chart using MSCombi2D.swf. The XML data is similar in structure to the multi-series chart. The three years that form the x-axis labels are provided as <category> elements. There are two data series in the chart, one representing the actual revenue, and the other, projected revenue. There are a few new attributes that we have added to the <dataset> element of the data series representing the projected revenue, as the following line of code:

```
<dataset seriesName='Projected Revenue' renderAs='Line' dashed='1'
   showValues='0' color='666666'>
```

The first attribute renderAs='Line' instructs FusionCharts to render this series as a line series. The other possible values are Column and Area for this chart. As this line in the chart reflects guidance of revenues, we have visually indicated this by plotting it as a dashed line using the attribute dashed='1'. Thereafter, we have turned off the display of the data values for this series using showValues='0' to avoid cluttering of too many data values. Finally, we have provided a custom color for this series using color='666666'.

Simple, isn't it? Let us now build the second type of combination chart, to compare the revenues versus units of products sold.

Time for action – a chart showing revenue versus units sold

1. Create a copy of `ActualVsProjected.html` in the same folder and name it `RevenueVsUnits.html`.

2. Change the reference of the chart SWF file in embedding code from `MSCombi2D.swf` to `MSCombiDY2D.swf`, to use a chart with dual axes.

3. Change the XML URL to `RevenueVsUnits.xml` in the chart embedding code.

4. Create an XML file with the name `RevenueVsUnits.xml` in the same folder and write the following data in it:

```
<chart caption='Harry&apos;s SuperMart' subcaption='Revenue and
  Units
  Sold by Year' xAxisName='Year' PYAxisName='Amount'
  SYAxisName='Units Sold' numberPrefix='$'>
  <categories>
    <category label='2009' />
    <category label='2010' />
    <category label='2011' />
  </categories>
  <dataset seriesName='Revenue'>
    <set value='1487500' />
    <set value='2100600' />
    <set value='2445400' />
  </dataset>
  <dataset seriesName='Units Sold' parentYAxis='S' renderAs='Line'
    showValues='0' color='666666'>
    <set value='24355' />
    <set value='38998' />
    <set value='43987' />
  </dataset>
</chart>
```

5. Open `RevenueVsUnits.xml` in your browser. You should see a chart similar to the following screenshot:

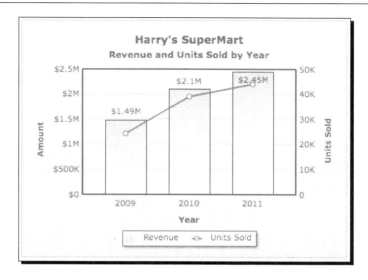

What just happened?

We just enabled Harry to compare the revenues of Harry's SuperMart for the last three years, along with the units sold. This chart gives him a perspective on how the revenues are affected by the units sold. Note how this chart has two y-axes, one on the left called primary axis, and one on the right called secondary axis. Each axis has its title defined using two new attributes of the `<chart>` element, PYAxisName for the primary axis, and SYAxisName for the secondary axis. The attribute YAxisName is not applicable to this chart as there is no common y-axis.

```
<chart caption='Harry&apos;s SuperMart' subcaption='Revenue and Units
    Sold by Year' xAxisName='Year' PYAxisName='Amount'
    SYAxisName='Units Sold' numberPrefix='$'>
```

The numberPrefix attribute gets applied to the primary axes. If we had to specify a number prefix for the secondary axes, we would use the attribute sNumberPrefix.

There are two data series in the chart, the first representing the revenue, and the other containing data on the units sold. The second series, representing quantity, has a new attribute parentYAxis='S' that lets you configure whether this data series is plotted against the primary axis (parentYAxis='P', by default) or the secondary axis (parentYAxis='S'). In our example, as the units sold is to be plotted against the secondary axis, on the right, we have set parentYAxis='S', the other attributes remaining the same as before.

```
<dataset seriesName='Units Sold' parentYAxis='S' renderAs='Line'
    showValues='0' color='666666'>
```

If you were using a 3D chart such as `MSColumn3DLineDY.swf`, the `renderAs` attribute is not required, as the chart can only plot columns on the primary axis and lines on the secondary. Just setting `parentYAxis='Y'` plots the data series as a line against the secondary y-axis.

Summary

In this chapter, we learned how to create the basic charts using FusionCharts that form the building blocks for a large dashboard or a reporting application.

Specifically, we covered:

- How easy it is to download and set up FusionCharts for your application.
- How to create a chart and different methods to provide data to the chart, either in XML or JSON format.
- Different types of charts having one or more series. Single series were created to compare revenues across multiple years. Multi-series charts were created to compare the breakdown of this revenue into two segments —food products and non-food products.
- Combination charts that let you plot multiple types of series on the same chart. We built examples to plot the actual revenues versus the projected revenues, and also the revenues versus the quantity sold.

Now that we've learned how to build charts, we are ready to explore detailed features offered by each chart and how to customize them to your needs, which is the topic of the next chapter.

2
Customizing your Chart

Now that you have created your first couple of charts, you must be curious to customize them both aesthetically and functionally. As charts are typically part of a larger application such as an internal reporting system or a CRM dashboard, it becomes necessary to bring the overall look and feel of the application to the charts as well. Also, the users of different applications vary widely bringing in the need for functional customization, while some of them can interpret complex figures in seconds, others need visual cues to understand their data better.

In this chapter, you will learn how to:

- Customize visuals of the chart including border, background, and font
- Control how numbers appear on the chart
- Add visual context to data such as target sales on a monthly sales chart using trend lines
- Personalize the chart by adding your logo and URL
- Make your charts cater to an international audience by using multilingual characters

Let's get started.

Know thy chart

Before we get down to customizing the charts, you need to know your charts a little better. We will look at the important elements of the chart to start with, and dive into the finer aspects as we go along.

The following screenshot shows how the chart background and canvas look in a 3D Column chart:

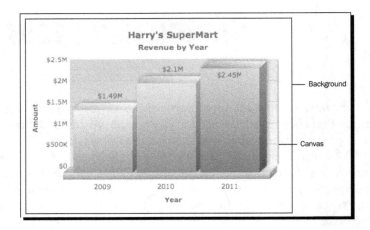

The following screenshot shows how it looks in a 2D Column chart:

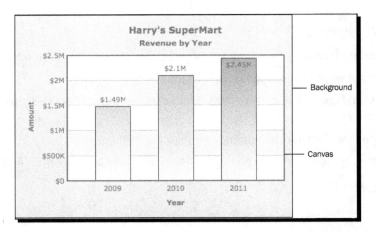

As you can see, the chart background refers to the entire *background* of the chart and the *canvas* refers to the area the chart is plotted in. The columns in a column chart, the lines in a line chart and the wedges (slices) in a pie chart are called **data plots**.

Now that we have got the basics in place, let's get started. Shall we?

Customizing the chart background

The chart background is the most prominent aesthetic element of the chart, and goes a long way in keeping the look of the chart in sync with the complete application. The 3D charts have a white background by default, and the 2D ones have a light gray one.

Just like you had set the chart caption using `<chart caption='Harry&apos;s SuperMart' ...>`, the background color is also customized using XML/JSON attributes of the `<chart>` element. We will be using XML examples throughout the chapter as they are more human-readable, and implementing them in JSON should be no rocket science.

Time for action – customizing the chart background

1. Create a folder called `CustomizingCharts` under `LearningFusionCharts`. This is the folder where we are going to store all the HTML and XML files for everything we learn in this chapter.

2. Copy the files `FirstChart.html` and `Data.xml` from the `FirstChart` folder, and rename them as `ChartBackground.html` and `ChartBackground.xml` respectively.

3. In `ChartBackground.html`, update the URL of the XML data file from `Data.xml` to `ChartBackground.xml` by setting the following parameter:

    ```
    myChart.setXMLUrl("ChartBackground.xml");
    ```

4. In `ChartBackground.xml`, add the attribute `bgColor='CCCCCC'` to the `<chart>` element as shown in the following lines of code:

    ```
    <chart bgColor='CCCCCC' caption='Harry&apos;s SuperMart'
      subcaption='Revenue by Year' xAxisName='Year' yAxisName='Amount'
      numberPrefix='$'>
    ```

5. When you open `FirstChart.html` in a browser, you will see the same 3D Column chart you had created earlier but with a dark gray background instead of the default white, as displayed in the following screenshot:

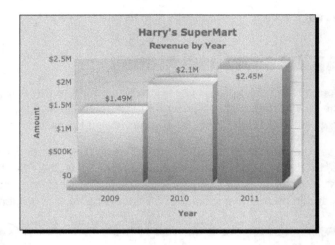

What just happened?

You have just taken your first step in the world of massive customization possibilities FusionCharts Suite offers. After making a copy of the first chart you created and changing the URL of the XML data file suitably, you changed the background color of the 3D Column chart from the default white to dark gray using `bgColor='CCCCCC'`. The attribute takes in a hex color code without the # symbol, and colors the background of the chart using it. In case you want a gradient background instead of a solid one, just add all the colors you want in the gradient to the attribute. For example, for a gradient having dark gray and white, you would need to set `bgColor='CCCCCC, FFFFFF'`.

Control the finer aspects of the gradient

When you assign multiple colors to the `bgColor` attribute to have a gradient background, there are times when you would want to control the ratio in which the colors are distributed in the gradient. With FusionCharts Suite, you have complete control over that as you do over the angle of the gradient and the transparency of the colors using simple attributes. You can learn more about these attributes in the online documentation at www.fusioncharts.com/docs | **Quick Chart Configuration** | **Chart Border & Background**. Or if you are working with a particular chart type, say the 3D Column chart, then you can learn about all the attributes it supports at www.fusioncharts.com/docs | **Chart XML API** | **Single Series Charts** | **Column 3D Chart** including the background. You can do this for any of the charts, or for any of the chart elements we discuss in this chapter.

Have a go hero – set a gradient fill for the canvas on a 2D Column chart

The background fill for the canvas works the same way as the chart background. You just need to prefix the attribute with canvas, so `bgColor` becomes `canvasBgColor`. Set a gradient background with these three colors , `b7bf4a` (light green), `ffeac0` (beige) and `f5b76a` (light orange). Note that this will work only for a 2D Column chart and not a 3D one as the 3D canvas takes in only one color for the canvas background, on top of which it applies a precalculated 3D lighting effect.

Image as chart background

You can also add personality to your charts by adding an image as the chart background— GIF, JPEG, PNG, or an SWF file. For example, you could use an image of currency notes as the background in a chart showing monthly revenue, or you could add a watermark to the charts in the trial version of your application. You must be careful not to overdo or misuse background images in your charts, as it can severely impact the readability of the chart.

Time for action – setting currency notes as the chart background

1. Create a copy of `ChartBackground.html` and `ChartBackground.xml`, and rename them to `ImageBackground.html` and `ImageBackground.xml` respectively. Also make the change in XML data URL.

2. Change the chart type to `Column2D.swf` in `ImageBackground.html` using the following line of code:

    ```
    var myChart = new FusionCharts("../FusionCharts/Column2D.swf",
       "myChartId", "400", "300", "0", "1" );
    ```

3. Find a nice background image with currency notes. You can either search for an image shared under the Creative Commons license at `http://search.creativecommons.org/` or use the beautiful image at `http://www.flickr.com/photos/amagill/3367543296/sizes/z/in/photostream/`. Save it as `money.jpg` in the `CustomizingCharts` folder.

4. Add the attribute `canvasbgAlpha='0'` to the `<chart>` element, and remove `bgColor='CCCCCC'`.

5. Add the attributes `bgImage='money.jpg'` `bgImageAlpha='30'` `bgImageDisplayMode='fit'`.

6. Open `ImageBackground.html` in a browser to see money sprayed behind the revenue figures in the chart, as shown in the following screenshot:

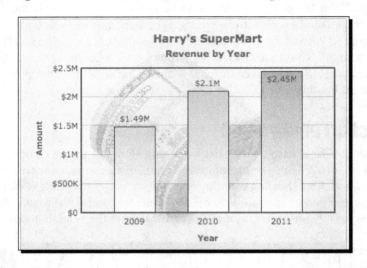

What just happened?

We changed the chart type to the 2D Column chart as it brings out the background image much better. In a 3D chart, the canvas would come in the way of the image and removing the canvas is not an option as that would leave the columns hanging in thin air. After finding a nice image to go with the chart, we removed the background color of the chart and made the canvas of the chart transparent to get a full view of the currency notes.

To add a background image, all we had to do was specify the relative path of the image to the `bgImage` attribute. Due to security restrictions, your image file has to reside on the same sub-domain as the chart file and a relative path to it has to be specified. Thereafter, we reduced the transparency of the image using `bgImageAlpha` so that it did not hinder the comprehensibility of the chart. Finally, to get the image to fit proportionately on the entire chart, we set `bgImageDisplayMode` to fit. There are other modes that you can select from as well: Stretch, Tile, Fill, and Center. You can either pick any of these modes or manually set the scaling and alignment of the images using the attributes discussed at `www.fusioncharts.com/docs` | **Quick Chart Configuration** | **Chart Border & Background**.

Customizing the chart border

By default, the 2D charts have a border around them and the 3D ones do not. To enable the border in a 3D chart, you just need to set `<chart showBorder='1'...>`. The border's color and thickness can then be customized using the `borderColor` and `borderThickness` attributes respectively.

The 2D charts have a border around the canvas too, which can be customized using the same attributes, just that you need to prefix the word `canvas` before them.

Customizing the data plot

Data plots, as we talked about earlier, are the columns in a column chart, the lines in a line chart, the wedges in a pie chart and similar. These data plots come with a lot of customization options and you can use them to highlight individual data points as well.

Customizing the color of the data plot

Each of the columns pick a different color by default in the column chart, and the same behavior is exhibited by the bar and the pie chart as well. The line and the area chart are drawn in the same color throughout. However, you can specify the color you want for each of the data plots in any of these charts by using the `color` attribute of the `<set>` element.

```
<set label='2009' value='1487500' color='FFFFDD'/>
```

You can use the data plot color to highlight a specific data point as well, say the highest revenue in a month, or the lowest, for that matter. It is one of the most commonly used data highlighting techniques wherein the data to be highlighted is given a unique color, while all the other columns have the same color, as you can see in the following screenshot:

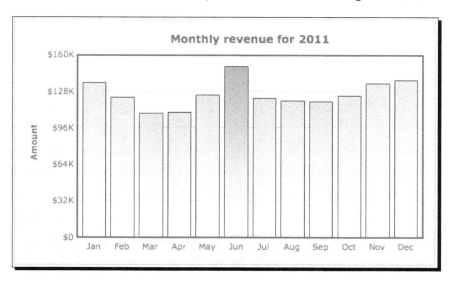

Different charts interpret the colors you define for the data plots differently, trying to make them look as good as possible. For example, the 3D Column chart takes a single color for the data plot and uses 3D lighting on top of that, while the 2D Column chart plots the columns using the color you specify with a default white gradient. These options (3D lighting and common gradient for all the plots) are controlled using attributes of the `<chart>` element. To switch off the 3D lighting, and get a solid color for all the columns in the 3D Column chart, just use `<chart use3DLighting='0'...>`. Similarly, to use a solid color in the 2D Column chart, that is, to remove the default white gradient that comes up, use `<chart plotGradientColor=''  ...>`. In case you want all the columns to gradient to some other color than the default white, you can set it globally for all the columns as well, using `plotGradientColor='333333'`.

Customizing the border of the data plot

The 2D Column chart, as you can see in the previous screenshot, has a border around each of the columns. In case you don't like the border, and want to turn it OFF, you can simply set `showPlotBorder='0'`. If you like the border but not the way it looks, you can customize its color and thickness globally, using the `plotBorderColor` and `plotBorderThickness` attributes respectively. You can also have a dashed border around the data plots by setting `<chart plotBorderDashed='1'...>`.

Having a dashed border around a data point is another way to highlight it. To do this, all you need to do is use `<set dashed='1'  ...>` for the column you want to highlight. The chart that you get will be similar to the following screenshot:

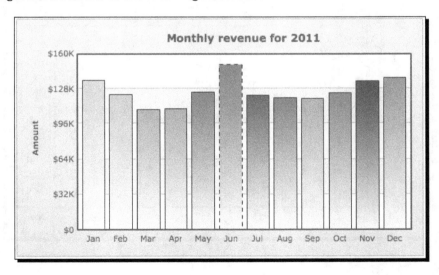

Have a go hero – highlight an anchor in a line chart

While you can highlight a data point in a line chart using `<set dashed='1'...>` similar to the 2D Column chart, it makes the line segment between that data point and the next one dashed, and could confuse the user as to which data point exactly is highlighted. To highlight a single data point, the best way is to give the anchor a different look from the other anchors. The attributes that govern the looks of an individual anchor are the same as the ones that govern them globally; just that one is for individual `<set>` elements and another for the global `<chart>` element – `anchorSides`, `anchorRadius`, `anchorBorderColor`, and `anchorBgColor`. It is usually a good idea to make the anchor highlighted a little bigger in size and darker in color than the other anchors. So go ahead, create a line chart showing the monthly revenue and highlight the month having the highest revenue.

Customizing the font properties

You can also customize the font face, size and color of all the text in the chart – captions, data labels, values, and so on. This is done using the `baseFont`, `baseFontSize`, and `baseFontColor` attributes all of which are self-explanatory.

All the text on the chart can be classified into two – the values and the tooltips inside the canvas, and all the labels and the captions outside it. There are times when you want to increase the font size of all the text on the chart but the chart can get a little cluttered when the size of the data values next to the data plots are increased as well. In such cases, you can selectively control only the text outside the canvas using the `outCnvBaseFont`, `outCnvBaseFontSize`, and `outCnvBaseFontColor` attributes. The outside canvas font properties override the base font properties for text outside the chart.

Configuring the y-axis and divisional lines

In all the charts that we have created until now, we just supplied the data and the chart automatically calculated the *lower* and *upper limits*. It also added divisional lines to help us in analyzing data – the horizontal lines that run through the chart at **$500K**, **$1M**, **$1.5M**, and the like, in all our charts. While the defaults work well in most cases, there are times when you would want to set the axis limits by hand and also the number of divisional lines.

Time for action – customizing the chart limits and the number of divisional lines

1. Create a copy of `ChartBackground.html` and `ChartBackground.xml`, and rename them to `ChartLimitCustomization.html` and `ChartLimitCustomization.xml` respectively. Make the change in XML data URL and remove the background attribute for all the forthcoming examples, wherever we make a copy of the chart background files, let's assume this step by default to keep our focus on the new stuff.

2. Add the attributes `adjustDiv='0' yAxisMaxvalue='3000000' numDivLines='2'` to the `<chart>` element.

3. Check out `ChartLimitCustomization.html` in a browser to see how the chart limits and the divisional lines are under your control now.

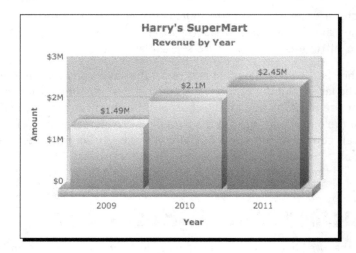

What just happened?

First up, as we wanted to explicitly specify the y-axis upper limit and the number of divisional lines, we had to disable automatic adjustment of divisional lines using `adjustDiv='0'`. It is pretty simple after that, we just set the y-axis upper limit using `yAxisMaxValue='3000000'`, and the number of divisional lines to 2 using `numDivLines='2'`. That's it, we are done.

Similar to the upper limit, you can also set the lower limit for the chart explicitly using the `yAxisMinValue` attribute. However, changing the lower limit to anything other than zero makes the differences in values appear much more than they actually are, and we don't recommend using it.

Does the y-axis look too cluttered? Skip some values.

In case you need a large number of divisional lines each with their corresponding values on the chart, the y-axis can get cluttered. As reducing the number of divisional lines is not an option, you can opt to skip every *n*th value on the y-axis using the `yAxisValuesStep` attribute. So if you set `yAxisValuesStep='2'`, every second value on the y-axis will be shown, skipping one in between.

Formatting the numbers on the chart

If you have noticed the numbers on the chart carefully, you would see 1490000 and 2100000 have been neatly converted to 1.49M and 2.1M respectively, thus making them much easier to read.

FusionCharts automatically formats the number scaling to convert to K (Thousands) and M (Millions). So if the values on your chart are 13300, 14500, and 10000, the chart will automatically convert them to 13.3K, 14.5K and 10K respectively. In case you don't want the numbers getting formatted this way, you can set `formatNumberScale='0'`. Once you do that, the numbers are displayed as 13,300, 14,500, and 10,000. Commas have been added to make the numbers easier to read. In case you don't want the commas either, you need to set `formatNumber='0'` as well.

Adding a prefix or suffix to the numbers

Throughout the examples in the book, we have been adding the $ prefix to all the numbers on the chart using `numberPrefix='$'`. Mostly, currency signs are prefixed to all the numbers on the chart in this way; however you can use it for anything you want to add before the numbers. Similarly, you can also add a suffix to all the numbers on the chart using the `numberSuffix` attribute. Typical uses would be the % sign or units such as mph and p.a. (per annum).

Configuring decimal places on the chart

You can control the decimal precision of all the numbers on the chart using the `decimals` attribute. For example, if the values on your chart are 12.432, 13.456, and 13 and you set `<chart ... decimals='2' >`, the numbers would be rounded off to 12.43, 13.46 and 13 respectively. You would notice that even though we have set the number of decimal places to two, no trailing zeroes are added after 13 to force it to have two decimal places. In case you want to force all the numbers to have the same decimal places using trailing zeroes, you need to use `forceDecimals='1'`. So the numbers would now become 12.43, 13.46 and 13.00 respectively. Note that if you have set `formatNumber='0'`, the formatting you have set for decimal places will not work.

Setting up your own number scale

We talked about how FusionCharts Suite uses the default number scale to convert the number to thousands and millions for easier readability. For a moment, let's assume that Harry's SuperMart is actually as big as Walmart, and the revenues are in billions instead of millions. When you are plotting the chart for the billionaire Harry, the data that you enter will be converted to millions but not billions. So we will have to define a custom number scale which understands the conversion to billions as well.

Time for action – setting up a number scale to understand billions as well

1. Create a copy of `ChartBackground.html` and `ChartBackground.xml`, and rename them to `CustomNumScale.html` and `CustomNumScale.xml` respectively.

2. Add the attributes `numberScaleValue='1000,1000,1000'` `numberScaleUnit='K,M,B'` to the `<chart>` element.

3. Add three zeroes to each of the three revenue figures so that the new number scale consisting of billions can kick in.

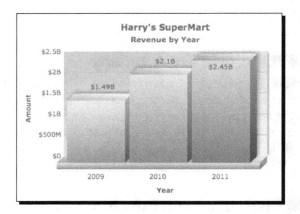

What just happened?

We just created a number scale to convert all the numbers in the chart to K, M, and B. Here's how the conversion works in simpler terms:

1000 = 1K

1000 K=1M

1000 M=1B

The same has been explained to the chart using `numberScaleValue='1000,1000,1000'` `numberScaleUnit='K,M,B'`. Essentially, what it means for the chart is, convert any number on the scale of 1000 to K, any number on the scale of 1000x1000 to M (the next value in `numberScaleUnit`), and any number on the scale of 1000x1000x1000 to B (the last value in `numberScaleUnit`). The only thing is that, as all the numbers on the chart are in the tune of billions, you don't get to see numbers in K and M. If Harry's revenue for 2009 and 2010 were 14875 and 2100600 respectively, the same number scale would have converted them to 14.88K and 2.1M respectively.

Have a go hero – create a number scale to convert seconds to minutes, hours, and days

The number scale we created in the previous example was more an extension of the default scale FusionCharts Suite already has. The real use of the custom number scale is when you need to define your own scales and the data in the chart varies pretty widely to actually need the different units defined in the scale. For example, in a chart plotting memory usage of a network server, it is very helpful to convert input data in bits to more easily understandable bytes, KBs, MBs, GBs, TBs, and more. Or in a chart plotting average support response time of different companies which is what you would be building here. The input data will be in seconds and you need to convert that to minutes, hours, and days. The numbers should look similar to the following table:

	Input data (seconds)	Output data using the number scale
Company A	430	7.17 min
Company B	2181	36.35 min
Company C	101012	1.17 day
Company D	1172	19.53 min

Customizing data labels and values on the chart

Data labels are the names of data points that appear on the x-axis, and **data values** are the values themselves that are displayed alongside the data plot. In case you don't want to display them, you can hide them using `showLabels='0'` and `showValues='0'` respectively. Both the label and the value will be displayed in the tooltip of the data plot even if you have hidden them. You can also opt to show the label of only selective data points to highlight it – first hide all of them and then display only the ones you want to, using `<set showLabel='1' ...>` for the respective data point. This can be done for data values as well using `<set showValue='1' ...>`.

Different modes to display data labels.

Quite often, the length of the labels is more than what can be accommodated in the space available to the chart. But don't you worry, all the charts come with intelligent label management to accommodate the labels in the smartest possible way. The charts also come with four modes of displaying the labels that you can pick from.

◆ **Wrap mode**: Long labels get wrapped in multiple lines. If there is not enough space to accommodate the complete label even with the wrapping, the chart trims them and adds ellipses at the end to indicate that they have been trimmed. The complete label can then be viewed in the tooltip. To set the wrap mode, all you need to do is set `<chart labelDisplay='WRAP'...>`, as shown in the following screenshot:

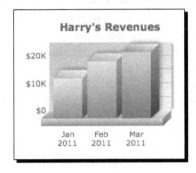

◆ **Rotate mode**: All labels get rotated vertically by setting `labelDisplay='Rotate'`, as shown in the following screenshot:

In case you think rotated labels are hampering readability, you can make them slanted by setting `labelDisplay='Rotate' slantLabels='1'`, as shown in the following screenshot:

- **Stagger mode**: The labels get distributed on multiple lines, which by default is 2. You need to set `labelDisplay='Stagger'`, and then, you can define the number of lines you want the labels staggered to using `staggerLines='n'`, as shown in the following screenshot:

- **Skip mode**: Skips every nth label, as defined by you. It should be used only when the labels represent something continuous and well known in nature such as date or time. To use this mode, use the `labelStep='n'` attribute, as shown in the following screenshot:

The default mode is called **Auto mode**, wherein the chart picks the better of the Wrap and Rotate mode.

Different modes to display data values

Data values, by default, are displayed horizontally. If you want values to be rotated, you can do that using `rotateValues='1'`.

In a column chart, you can also opt to display the labels inside the columns using the `placeValuesInside='1'` attribute. It can be combined with `rotateValues` to have rotated figures inside the columns.

Add details to your chart using custom labels instead of data values

If you want to explain the sudden increase or fall in the revenue of a particular year, you can do that on the chart itself using custom labels. You just need to use `<set displayValue='Year End Discount, $42.3K' ...>` and the label will be shown on the chart instead of the data value.

Configuring the tooltips

Every time you hover over a data plot, a tooltip with the name and the value of that point will come up. In case you don't want to have tooltips on your chart, you can switch it off using `showToolTip='0'`.

On the other hand, you can use the tooltip to show added details about the data points, which if present on the chart can add a lot of clutter to it. To have a custom tooltip instead of the default name and value, you need to use `<set tooltext='Detailed explanation comes here' ...>`. You can also break down the tooltip into multiple lines using `{br}`. So if we wanted to add more details to Harry's revenue chart, the tooltip could be:

```
<set label='2009' value='1487500' toolText='Apparels:
  27%{br}Household: 37%{br}Electronic Goods: 19%{br}Sports and
  Fitness: 17%'/>
```

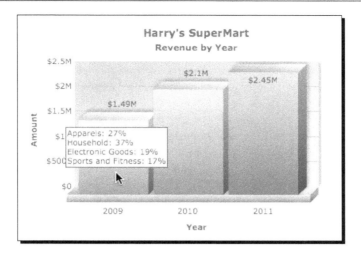

Configuring the legend in multi-series charts

When you created your first multi-series chart, you must have seen that the legend at the bottom of the chart helps identify the series name. The legend comes up in all multi-series and combination charts by default.

The user can click on the icon for a data series to hide it and focus on the other series. To bring it back, the user just needs to click on the icon again. The interactivity comes in really handy when you have a number of series plotted on the chart, and the user just wants to focus on a particular series.

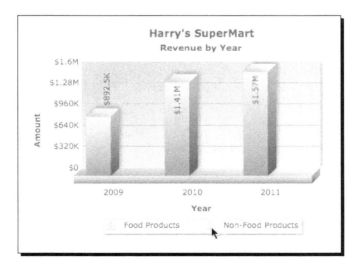

Similar to the other chart elements, even the legend is highly customizable, both aesthetically and functionally. By default, the legend is shown at the bottom of the chart. However, if you prefer it on the right, you need to set `<chart legendPosition='RIGHT'...>`. To learn more about how to customize the legend aesthetically, please check out `www.fusioncharts.com/docs` | **Quick Chart Configuration** | **Legend**.

Pie and doughnut charts have the legend too

The pie and the doughnut chart are the only single-series charts that have the option of displaying the legend. In order to enable the legend, you just need to set `<chart showLegend="1"...>`. The interactivity of the legend is completely opposite to the multi-series and combination charts, though every time the user clicks on an item in the legend, the respective wedge slices out thus bringing it into focus.

Adding a trendline to the chart

Trendlines help you add more meaning to the chart, by helping the user view the data in context to some pre-determined value. For example, trendlines can be used to show the target in a monthly revenue chart or mark out the critical zone for a chart monitoring the temperature of a nuclear reactor.

Time for action – adding a trendline to show target revenue

1. Create a copy of `ChartBackground.html` and `ChartBackground.xml`, and rename them to `Trendline.html` and `Trendline.xml` respectively.

2. Add the following code to `Trendline.xml` right after the chart data:

    ```
    <trendLines>
      <line startValue='430000' color='009933'
        displayvalue='Target' />
    </trendLines>
    ```

3. Open `Trendline.html` in a browser.

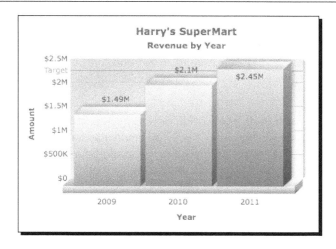

What just happened?

Your chart can have multiple trendlines on a chart, so they need to be enclosed within the `<trendlines></trendlines>` tags. For each trendline, you need a `<line>` element. We then defined its start value, color and the label to be displayed alongside the trendline. In case your trendline needs to have a different end value, you can define that as well using the `endValue` attribute that would result in a slanted trendline.

Have a go hero – add a trendzone to the chart

Trendzones are similar to trendlines, except that they mark out a range, and hence, necessarily need a start value and an end value. Also, to tell the chart you are creating a trendzone, just add `isTrendZone='1'` to the `<line>` element. Convert the trendline to a trendzone setting whatever target you would like for Harry and his team.

Personalizing the chart

Personalizing your charts helps add credibility especially when you are packaging them to an external audience. With FusionCharts Suite, you can add your logo to the chart and have your own link in the context menu (right-click menu).

Time for action – adding a logo and link to the chart

1. Create a copy of `ChartBackground.html` and `ChartBackground.xml`, and rename them to `PersonalizedChart.html` and `PersonalizedChart.xml` respectively.

2. Get a logo that you think works well for Harry's SuperMart and place it under `CustomizingCharts` as `logo.jpg`. You could also have the logo in GIF/PNG/SWF format. The logo has to reside on the same subdomain as the chart files. In case you can't find a suitable logo, pick up this **H** sign from `http://www.flickr.com/photos/hansdorsch/2759771921/sizes/o/in/photostream/` shared under the Creative Commons license.

3. Add the following attributes to the `<chart>` element: `logoURL='logo.jpg' logoPosition='TL' logoScale='10' logoAlpha='60' logoLink='http://www.harryssupermart.com'`.

4. Also add `aboutMenuItemLabel='About Harry&apos;s SuperMart' aboutMenuItemLink='http://www.harryssupermart.com'`.

5. Open the page in a browser to check out the new personalized chart. Right-click on it to see the about menu item showing **About Harry's SuperMart**.

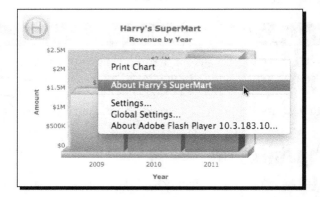

What just happened?

`logoURL` takes in the relative URL of the logo to be loaded at runtime. Then we specified the position of the logo as `TL`, that is, top-left corner of the chart. The other positions you can pick from are `TR` (top-right), `BL` (bottom-left), `BR` (bottom-right), and `CC` (center of the chart). The logo was pretty big in size, so we reduced it using the `logoScale` attribute. Also, to make sure that the logo did not distract from the chart itself while keeping the branding in place, we reduced its opacity using `logoAlpha`. We also linked the logo to Harry's SuperMart's website using the `logoLink` attribute.

To customize the about menu item, we just needed to use the `aboutMenuItemLabel` and `aboutMenuItemLink` attributes, the first of which sets the label that you see on the menu (and replaces the default About FusionCharts label) and the second one, the link itself.

Using multilingual characters on the chart

If you cater to an international audience, wouldn't you like your charts in the reports and dashboards to be in the language of your audience? FusionCharts Suite allows you to use **multilingual (UTF-8) characters** on the charts, so your charts can go international too.

To use multilingual characters on the chart, you need to use UTF-8 encoded XML and the XML file/stream requires a **Byte Order Mark (BOM) stamp** to be present as the very first 3 bytes of the file. BOM is an indicator that the file contains UTF-8 encoded strings. Adding the BOM stamp is simple, and it depends upon the method you are using to provide data to the chart.

Adding the BOM stamp in the Data URL method

As we learned in the *Chapter 1*, *Introducing FusionCharts*, the method by which we provide a URL to the chart to get data from (either a static XML file or data relayed by a stream) is called the Data URL method. This is the method we have been using throughout this chapter to pass data to the chart.

When you are using a static XML file (as we have done throughout the chapter), you can manually insert the BOM stamp to the XML data file following these 3 steps:

1. Open the file in a text editor that supports UTF-8 encoding with BOM stamp (Notepad on Windows or TextEdit on Mac).

2. Open the save menu and specify the filename, file type, encoding and BOM mark (if the option is available).

3. Save the file.

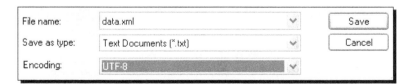

Typically, you wouldn't have a static XML file passing data to the chart in real-life business applications. You will instead have server side scripts virtually relaying the XML data document to the chart, as we will explore later. In that case, you can use either of the following methods:

- **Manually add BOM to the XML relayer script file**: Similar to adding BOM stamp to the static XML files you can also add the BOM stamp to the server side file which would be relaying the dynamically generated XML. This needs to be done when the file has just been created.

- **Write BOM using script**: In most cases, the file relaying the XML would have been created with ANSI-encoded format. In that case, you need to add the BOM using the script at the very beginning of the output stream. To append BOM in a PHP page, you would need the following code:

```
header ( 'Content-type: text/xml' );
echo pack ( 'C3 , 0xef, 0xbb, 0xbf' );
```

To implement BOM stamp with other server-side technologies, head to www.fusioncharts.com/docs | **Advanced Charting** | **Using Special Characters** | **Using Multi-lingual text**.

Adding the BOM stamp in the Data String method

Similar to adding the BOM stamp to a static XML file, you will need to save the file containing the chart SWF and XML with the BOM stamp. Again, this needs to be done when the file has just been created.

Changing chart messages

Having created so many charts, by now you must have seen the **Loading Chart** or **Retrieving Data** message at least once. Or maybe the **Invalid data** message when you missed something in the XML. All of these messages are customizable too and you can have anything you want, to keep the messaging style the same throughout your application, or to add your own touch to them. All the messages are controlled by the attributes that you need to set in the page that renders the chart.

Attribute name	What does it set a message for?	Default value
PBarLoadingText	When the chart is loading	**Loading Chart. Please Wait.**
XMLLoadingText	When the data is loading	**Retrieving Data. Please Wait.**
ParsingDataText	When the data is being parsed	**Retrieving Data. Please Wait.**

Attribute name	What does it set a message for?	Default value
ChartNoDataText	When there is no data for the chart to display or the chart hasn't got data in the structure it expects, for example sending multi-series data to a single-series chart	**No data to display.**
RenderingChartText	When the chart is being drawn	**Rendering Chart. Please Wait.**
LoadDataErrorText	When the URL provided for fetching the data from is invalid or inaccessible	**Error in loading data.**
InvalidXMLText	When the data is invalid as per XML validation rules	**Invalid data.**

Time for action – changing the Invalid data message

1. Create a copy of `ChartBackground.html` and `ChartBackground.xml`, and rename them to `CustomChartMessage.html` and `CustomChartMessage.xml` respectively.

2. Open `CustomChartMessage.html` and add the following highlighted line of code in it:

```
<div id="chartContainer">FusionCharts will load here!</div>
<script type="text/javascript"><!--  var myChart =
  new FusionCharts("../FusionCharts/Column3D.swf", "myChartId",
  "400", "300", "0", "1" );
  myChart.setXMLUrl("ChartBackground.xml");
  myChart.configure("InvalidXMLText", "The world has a new order.
    This chart shall not render.");
  myChart.render("chartContainer");// -->
</script>
```

3. Open `CustomChartMessage.xml` and mess up the XML. Don't be too destructive, removing a closing > will do the trick too.

4. Open `CustomChartMessage.html` in a browser and see how the world has a new order.

> The world has a new order. This chart shall not render.

What just happened?

We modified the default message of the `InvalidXMLText` attribute. After the chart has been created, but before it has been rendered, we call `configure()` and pass it two values, first, the attribute we want to customize, and secondly, the new message. That's it!

In case you are setting multiple attributes at the same time, you can either call `configure()` multiple times, or call it once and pass it an object where each message type is the property name and custom message, the value.

```
myChart.configure( {
  "InvalidXMLText"  : " The world has a new order. This chart shall
    not render.",
  "ChartNoDataText" : "I have looked everywhere but there is just no
    data for me to show"
});
```

Summary

In this chapter, we took a deep dive into the massive customization possibilities FusionCharts Suite offers. Specifically, we learned how to:

◆ Customize the visuals of the chart such as background, border, and the data plots themselves

◆ Highlight data points using the customization properties available for individual data points

◆ Format numbers on the chart and define our own number scales

◆ Add context to the chart using trendlines and trendzones

◆ Add multilingual characters to the chart by adding the BOM stamp

◆ Customizing the chart messages by calling `configure()` before rendering the chart

In the next chapter, we will look at the tight integration between FusionCharts Suite and JavaScript, how that can be used to manipulate charts at client-side, and add better printing support.

3
JavaScript Capabilities

Harry has set up a quick weekly audit process for three departments in his SuperMart. Positive move indeed! But, what use is an audit if there is no report at the end of it all? Thus, on came the request to set up a page just for this.

It quickly dawned upon us that we would need to make the audit report more useful than if it were merely displaying a set of charts. We will add functionalities to the page that will make his report viewing experience more comprehensive during daily use. "More comprehensive" means ensuring the charts load really fast, be seamlessly printed, and have the ability to easily copy the data to spreadsheets.

For adding these functionalities we will make use of JavaScript capabilities of FusionCharts.

In this chapter, we shall:

- ◆ Access charts using JavaScript
- ◆ Learn how to use JavaScript events raised by the charts
- ◆ Dynamically update a chart's data without reloading the page or the chart
- ◆ Retrieve data from a chart in XML, JSON, and CSV formats
- ◆ Manipulate chart cosmetics using JavaScript
- ◆ Make charts print better across browsers using managed printing
- ◆ Learn how to track errors and debug charts using JavaScript

Before you start using the JavaScript capabilities of FusionCharts, you will require basic concepts of programming in JavaScript. `http://www.w3schools.com/js/` is a great resource to start learning JavaScript online.

Access your charts using JavaScript

For us to implement any of the previously mentioned functionalities, we will first need to access the FusionCharts JavaScript object. We call this the **chart object**. The chart object consists of a number of functions and variables that allow us to programmatically communicate with the charts.

In *Chapter 1, Introducing FusionCharts*, we executed the statement `var myChart = new FusionCharts("../FusionCharts/Column2D.swf", "myChartId", "400", "300", "0", "1")`, to create our first chart. The object that got stored within the `myChart` variable was the chart object itself. However, to implement the audit report page, we will look into other methods to access the chart object.

Time for action – setting up the audit report page

In the audit report page, we will first create a chart which has weekly sales data for one of the departments.

1. Under the `LearningFusionCharts` folder that we had earlier created in *Chapter 1, Introducing FusionCharts*, create a new folder `JavaScriptCapabilities`. This will store all the files that we will incrementally create in this chapter.

2. Create a new file `AccessingChart.html` and type the following content into it:

```html
<html>
  <head>
    <title>Audit Report of Harry&apos;s SuperMart</title>
    <script type="text/javascript"
      src="../FusionCharts/FusionCharts.js">
    </script>
    <script type="text/javascript"><!--
      var myChart = new FusionCharts ("../FusionCharts/Column3D.
      swf",
        "myChartId", "400", "300", "0", "1");
      myChart.setXMLUrl("WeeklyApparelsSale.xml");
      function loadReport () {
        var chart = FusionCharts("myChartId");
        chart.render("chartContainer");}
      // -->
    </script>
  </head>
  <body onload="loadReport()">
    <div id="chartContainer">FusionCharts will load here!</div>
  </body>
</html>
```

3. Create an XML file in this folder with the name `WeeklyApparelsSale.xml` and type the following data in it:

```
<chart caption='Harry&apos;s SuperMart'
  subcaption='This week&apos;s sale of Apparels'
    xAxisName='Day of the week'
      yAxisName='Amount' numberPrefix='$'>
  <set label='Sun' value='18900' />
  <set label='Mon' value='13400' />
  <set label='Tue' value='10300' />
  <set label='Wed' value='7600' />
  <set label='Thu' value='14700' />
  <set label='Fri' value='16500' />
  <set label='Sat' value='22600' />
</chart>
```

4. Open `AccessingChart.html` in your browser and you should see the chart as shown in the following screenshot:

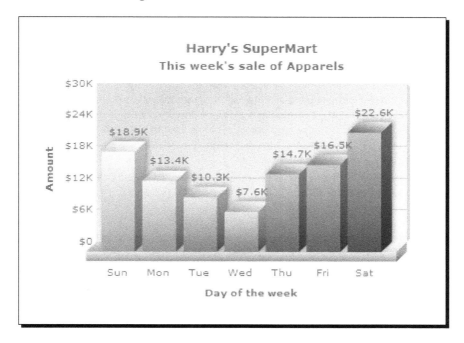

What just happened?

For the audit report page, instead of writing the code to create the chart inside the page <body>, we shifted the code to the <head>. Rendering the chart is not possible within the page <head> because the <body> element has not yet loaded. Thus, we created a function called `loadReport` with codes to render the chart. Finally, we added `onload="loadReport()"` to the <body> tag in order to execute this function when the page loads completely.

The statement `var chart = FusionCharts("myChartId")`, within the `loadReport` function, retrieved a reference of the chart that we had initially created on the page. We identified the chart to be accessed by using the chart ID, `myChartId`, which had been originally used while creating the chart. The key difference between creating a chart and accessing it back at a later time is to use a unique ID for identification of the chart. Simply removing the `new` keyword that we used while creating a chart and replacing all parameters with a single `chartId` parameter causes the FusionCharts object to return an already created chart instead of creating a new chart.

Once we accessed the chart object, the chart was rendered by executing the `render()` function.

Iterating through all charts on a page

There may be instances where we need to loop through all charts that are rendered within a page and interact programmatically with them. You can do this by iterating through the `FusionCharts.items` object. The `FusionCharts.items` object contains a list of all charts that have been created on the page and have not been deleted (disposed) yet. The charts are accessible here using their IDs.

For example, if you intend to access an already rendered chart having `myChartId` as ID, you will be required to write `FusionCharts.items["myChartId"]`.

Pop quiz – know your chart object

1. Which of the following lines of code returns the reference to a chart that has been already created?

    a. `var myChart = new FusionCharts ("column2D.swf", "myChartID");`

    b. `var myChart = FusionCharts ("myChartID");`

Listening to chart events

To meet our immediate purpose of adding interactive functionalities that we have planned for the audit report page, we will require a set of HTML form controls such as buttons and drop-down lists to appear below the chart. We will keep these items initially hidden and show them after the chart is completely visible. This ensures that these items always have an actual chart to work with.

For this to happen, we will need the help of chart events.

There are several events that are raised by FusionCharts during the lifetime of the chart on a page. These events, such as the chart completing its loading process or the chart not being able to load data, may be of interest to you. You might want to perform some action when such events occur. Each of these events have a unique name and FusionCharts provides two mechanisms for intercepting and reacting to them:

◆ The simple event model

◆ The advanced event model

The simple event model

In the simple event model, whenever an event occurs on a chart, it looks for a function defined on the page with the same name as that of the event. If one such function is found in the global (`window`) scope, the chart executes it.

Time for action – show chart controls when a chart is fully rendered

To show the area on the audit report page that will contain the chart controls, we listen to the `FC_Rendered` event that is fired when a chart completes the rendering process.

1. Create a copy of `AccessingChart.html` in the `JavaScriptCapabilities` folder and name it as `SimpleEvents.html`.

2. Make the following changes in the code of this file to add a new function called `FC_Rendered` and an HTML `<div>` element that will contain the chart controls:

   ```
   <html>
     <head>
       <title>Audit Report of Harry&apos;s SuperMart</title>
       <script type="text/javascript"
         src="../FusionCharts/FusionCharts.js">
       </script>
       <script type="text/javascript"><!--
        var myChart =
   ```

```
      new FusionCharts ("../FusionCharts/Column3D.swf",
      "myChartId", "400", "300", "0", "1");
      myChart.setXMLUrl("WeeklyApparelsSale.xml");
      function loadReport () {
        var chart = FusionCharts("myChartId");
        chart.render("chartContainer");
      }
      function FC_Rendered (chartId) {
        if (chartId == "myChartId") {
          document.getElementById("chartControls")
            .style.display = "block";
        }
      }
      // -->
    </script>
  </head>
  <body onload="loadReport()">
    <div id="chartContainer">FusionCharts will load here!</div>
    <div id="chartControls" style="display: none;">
      Chart controls will appear here.
    </div>
  </body>
</html>
```

3. Open this file in your browser and you should see that when the chart completes its animation, the placeholder text for your chart controls will be visible. In case this text does not become visible while you are running the XML locally (as `file://`), ensure that your Flash Global Security Settings are correctly set. You can visit `http://goto.fusioncharts.com/flash-global-security-settings-guide` for a step-by-step guide.

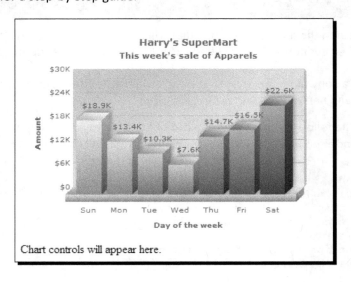

What just happened?

We added a new function called `FC_Rendered` that matches with the "`FC_Rendered`" event name of FusionCharts. We ensured that the function was in the global (window) scope in order to be accessible by the charts. When the chart completed its rendering process, it looked up for the presence of this function and executed it.

We added another HTML `<div>` element below the chart container and provided it with ID `chartControls`. We hid the element on the initial load by providing `display:none` to its `style` attribute. The event listener function `FC_Rendered` accessed this element using the ID and set its display style-property to `block`—consequently making the placeholder text for the chart controls visible.

> When charts raise events, they pass on certain parameters to the event listening function. The first parameter is always the ID of the chart that has raised the event. Under a page that has multiple charts, this helps in identifying which chart has raised this event.
>
> Certain events have additional parameters that are specific for that event. Details on arguments for each event can be located under the **FusionCharts & JavaScript | API Reference | Events** section of the product documentation.

Other than the `FC_Rendered` event that we encountered previously, there are more than a dozen other events that can be listened to and utilized. Some useful ones are listed in the following table:

Event Name	When does it occur?
FC_Loaded	The chart has completed loading itself within the browser
FC_DataLoaded	The data provided to the chart has been loaded successfully when fetched from an URL
FC_Rendered	The chart has processed the data and has successfully rendered the chart
FC_NoDataToDisplay	The chart has successfully loaded and processed the XML or JSON data, but was unable to render a chart due to a lack of computable data
FC_DataXMLInvalid	The chart could not successfully parse the XML or JSON provided to it due to malformed syntax of the data
FC_DataLoadError	The chart could not fetch data from a particular URL due to a network error, server error or invalid URL

The advanced event model

The simple event model is enough, as the name suggests, for *simple* use. In comparison, the advanced event model provides a uniform and highly standardized pattern of event tracking. This method of event handling takes the pain out of certain complexities and limitations of the simple event model.

If you have already used event handling on HTML elements, the advanced event model will make you feel at home. The `addEventListener` function on every chart allows you to add event listeners in a fashion similar to the `addEventListener` function (or the `attachEvent` function of Internet Explorer) on HTML elements.

The beauty of this model lies with the fact that, instead of having one single listener per event for all your charts on a page, you can track events separately for individual charts. You can even attach multiple listeners to the same event.

Time for action – replace simple events with the advanced event model

For a pure academic purpose, we would replace our previously used `FC_Rendered` simple event with its counterpart in the advanced event model.

1. Create a copy of `SimpleEvents.html` in the `JavaScriptCapabilities` folder and name it as `AdvancedEvents.html`.

2. Open this file in a text editor and replace the entire `FC_Rendered` function block (line number 17 through 22) with the following lines of code:

    ```
    function showChartControls() {
      document.getElementById("chartControls")
      .style.display = "block";
    }

    myChart.addEventListener("rendered", showChartControls);
    ```

3. Open this file in your browser and you should see that the chart controls' placeholder text shows up in a similar fashion to the earlier simple event model.

What just happened?

Instead of declaring functions with the exact same name as the event name, we created a very straightforward function, `showChartControls`, which does behave exactly as named! Then we called the `addEventListener` function of the chart and passed the event name and this function.

The addEventListener function accepts two parameters. The first is a string specifying the event type and the second is a function (or a reference to a function) that has to be executed.

 Similar to the simple event model, you can even attach event listeners across all the charts on your page using the advanced model itself. For that, the addEventListener method is also available on the FusionCharts constructor object and can be used in the usual fashion. FusionCharts. addEventListener("rendered", doSomething) will execute the function referred by doSomething when any chart renders on the page.

Event arguments in the advanced model

Advanced events have a very uniform argument pattern. All event listeners in the advanced model receive two parameters, eventType and eventArgs as objects.

The eventType object comprises of information pertaining to the chart that raised the event. The structure of the eventType parameter object is uniform across all events:

Variable Name	What does it contain?
eventId	Specifies a unique ID for the particular instance of this event
eventType	The name of the event
sender	Reference to the chart that raised the event
stopPropagation()	If multiple listeners are tracking the same event, executing this method within one such listener causes the following listeners to fail to execute

The second parameter, eventArgs, varies for each event type and contains information specific to the particular event. Details on this are available under the **FusionCharts & JavaScript | API Reference | Events** section of the product documentation.

Pop quiz – know when to use the advanced event model

1. What can you NOT do with the simple event model?

    a. Execute multiple functions on a single event

    b. Listen to events only from a particular chart on a page having multiple charts

    c. Both of the above

    d. Neither of the above

Dynamically updating chart data

The report page that we have currently developed shows the data of one single department of Harry's SuperMart. However, as per plan, Harry would review the daily sales of not one, but three of his departments at the end of every week. That means three different charts!

Putting up three different charts on a single page would defeat the whole purpose of showing charts for the report. A quick tip from Harry solved our problem. Harry informed us that he was not interested in comparing the performance between departments. Instead, he was more interested in tracking how each department individually performed on each day of the week. This implied that we could show the three charts on three different pages, one at a time.

Knowing that having a page for each department is slow to browse and also takes more time to develop, we would develop the audit page with a single chart and dynamically update its data.

Time for action – change chart data on the click of a button

We create a button to replace the chart's data with that of another department.

1. Create a copy of `AdvancedEvents.html` in the `JavaScriptCapabilities` folder and name it as `DynamicDataUpdate.html`.

2. Open this new file in a text editor and replace the text `Chart controls will appear here` (on line number 30) with the following HTML:

```
<p>
  <input type="button" onclick="updateData()"
    value="Show data of &quot;cosmetics&quot; department" />
</p>
```

3. Now, near the beginning of the page, look for the line of code (around line number 22) `myChart.addEventListener("rendered", showChartControls)`, and on the next line of it add a new line and insert the following snippet of code:

```
function updateData () {
  var chart = FusionCharts("myChartId");
  chart.setXMLUrl("WeeklyCosmeticsSale.xml");
}
```

4. Create a new XML file in this folder with the name `WeeklyCosmeticsSale.xml` and type the following data in it:

```
<chart caption='Harry&apos;s SuperMart'
 subcaption='This week&apos;s sale of Cosmetics'
    xAxisName='Day of the week'
      yAxisName='Amount' numberPrefix='$'>
    <set label='Sun' value='26100' />
    <set label='Mon' value='21900' />
    <set label='Tue' value='15500' />
    <set label='Wed' value='22300' />
    <set label='Thu' value='17100' />
    <set label='Fri' value='17200' />
    <set label='Sat' value='25200' />
</chart>
```

5. Open the `DynamicDataUpdate.html` file in your browser and you should see that when the chart completely renders, instead of the chart controls' placeholder text, we now see a button, as shown in the following screenshot:

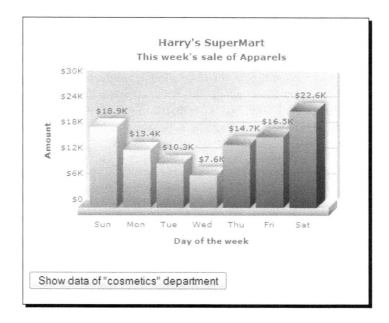

6. Click the button and the apparels sales data changes to cosmetics sales data, as shown in the following screenshot:

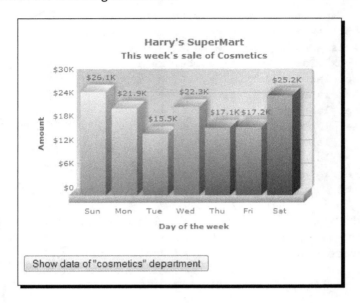

What just happened?

Once you set new data to a chart that you had previously rendered, you do not need to call the `render` function on the chart again. This is because the chart has already been rendered in the location we had previously specified and the only thing being changed is the data. Simply, passing on the new data using any data-setting function such as `setXMLData`, `setXMLUrl`, `setJSONData`, or `setJSONUrl` will do the trick.

The `updateData` function, very similar to the `loadReport` function, accesses the chart using its ID. The new button that we added within the "chartControls" `<div>` executes this function and updates the chart data by calling `setXMLUrl` on it using the URL of a new XML file.

Now that we have successfully updated the data of the chart without reloading the page, we complete adding the functionality to load data for the rest of the departments.

Having three buttons to update three sets of data would again be very clumsy. Thus, we would replace the button with a drop-down list from where we can select the data to load.

Time for action – update chart data from a drop-down list

1. Create a copy of `DynamicDataUpdate.html` in the `JavaScriptCapabilities` folder and name it as `DynamicDataUpdate2.html`.

2. Open this new file in a text editor and change the button text `Show data of &quot;cosmetics&quot; department` (around line number 37) to `Change Department`. Essentially, we made the button a bit more generic.

3. Find the line of HTML `<input type="button" onclick="updateData()"` (around line number 36), and just before it, insert a new line and type the following snippet of HTML to add a drop-down list:

```
<select id="departmentList">
  <option value="WeeklyApparelsSale.xml"
    selected="selected">Apparels Department</option>
  <option value="WeeklyCosmeticsSale.xml">
    Cosmetics Department</option>
  <option value="WeeklyElectronicsSale.xml">
    Electronics Department</option>
</select>
```

4. Within the `<head>` of the page, replace the entire `updateData` function definition (line number 23 through 26) with the following code:

```
function updateData () {
  var chart = FusionCharts("myChartId"),
    selectList = document.getElementById("departmentList"),
    dataUrl = selectList.options[selectList.selectedIndex].value;
  chart.setXMLUrl(dataUrl);
}
```

5. Create a new (third) XML file called `WeeklyElectronicsSale.xml` and type in the following XML data:

```
<chart caption='Harry&apos;s SuperMart'
  subcaption='This week&apos;s sale of Electronics'
    xAxisName='Day of the week'
    yAxisName='Amount' numberPrefix='$'>
  <set label='Sun' value='28300' />
  <set label='Mon' value='17800' />
  <set label='Tue' value='11900' />
  <set label='Wed' value='5300' />
  <set label='Thu' value='12200' />
  <set label='Fri' value='26500' />
  <set label='Sat' value='21100' />
</chart>
```

6. Open the `DynamicDataUpdate2.html` file using a browser and you notice that now we have a drop-down list below the chart. Select **Electronics Department** from the drop-down list and click on the **Change Department** button next to it. You should see the chart fetch new data and render this.

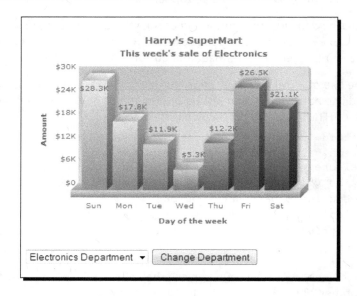

What just happened?

We added a drop-down list of departments that are part of this audit process and modified the `updateData` function to look up which item is currently selected in this list. For the value of each item in the drop-down list, we stored the filenames of the FusionCharts data XML corresponding to each department. We accessed this information with the line `selectList.options[selectList.selectedIndex].value`, and made the chart load the XML file for the selected item in the drop-down.

Retrieve data from chart

To help Harry better analyze the audit report, we decided to provide him with the functionality to sort the columns within the chart. One of the ways to provide this feature is to store the XMLs in sorted order. However, this method would be laborious as there needs to be three sets of data XML for each chart, one sorted ascending, the next sorted descending, and then the original one. Thus, we decided to make the sorting function dynamic and not create additional sets of XMLs.

FusionCharts allows us to fetch the data from the chart using any of the data-getting functions such as `getXMLData`, `getJSONData`, and `getDataAsCSV`.

Time for action – retrieve data from the chart and sort them

1. Create a copy of `DynamicDataUpdate2.html` in the `JavaScriptCapabilities` folder and name it as `SortChartData.html`.

2. Open this new file in a text editor. Insert the following HTML on a new line after the end of the paragraph element `</p>`, which contains the drop-down list (around line number 45):

```html
<p>
  <input type="button" onClick="sortData()"
    value="Sort Chart Data" />
</p>
```

3. Now, within the `<head>` of the page, add a new line after the end of the `updateData function` (around line number 28) and insert the following code:

```javascript
var descendingSort = true;
function sortData () {
  var chart = FusionCharts("myChartId"),
  chartData = chart.getJSONData();
  if (descendingSort) {
    chartData.data.sort(function (a, b) {
      return Number(a.value) < Number (b.value);
    });
  }
  else {
    chartData.data.sort(function (a, b) {
      return Number(a.value) > Number (b.value);
    });
  }
  chart.setJSONData(chartData);
  descendingSort = !descendingSort;
}
```

4. Open the `SortChartData.html` file in a browser and when the **Sort Chart Data** button is visible, as shown in the following screenshot, click on it:

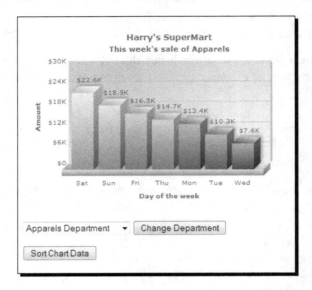

What just happened?

We added a button marked as **Sort Chart Data** and coded it to execute a function on click. We named the aforementioned function as `sortData` and defined it within the `<script>` block we were previously working on inside the `<head>` of the HTML.

Within this `sortData` function we used a nice little trick. Instead of fetching the data in the original XML format, we retrieved it as JSON. In FusionCharts JSON format, the data for the plot is specified as an array with the name `data`. Each element within the array is in turn an object with the label and value. A sample of the JSON that will be returned when we execute `chart.getJSONData()` will look similar to the following code:

```
{
  "chart": {
    "caption": "Harry's SuperMart",
    "subcaption": "This week's sale of Apparels",
    "xaxisname": "Day of the week",
    "yaxisname": "Amount",
    "numberprefix": "$"
  },
  "data": [
    { "label": "Sun", "value": "18900" },
```

```
        { "label": "Mon", "value": "13400" },
        { "label": "Tue", "value": "10300" },
        { "label": "Wed", "value": "7600" },
        { "label": "Thu", "value": "14700" },
        { "label": "Fri", "value": "16500" },
        { "label": "Sat", "value": "22600" }
    ]
}
```

We thus have the convenience of simply sorting this array using a JavaScript array's native `sort` method.

Pop quiz – do you recall the JSON data API?

1. Which is the function to set data to a chart object (say `myChartObj`) in JSON format?

   a. `myChartObj.setChartDataJSON()`

   b. `myChartObj.setDataAsJSON()`

   c. `myChartObj.setJSONData()`

Retrieving chart data as comma-separated values

It would be very useful for Harry if we allow him to easily copy the data, displayed on the chart, onto a spreadsheet. For that, we would add a button to the audit report page that will show the data in **Comma-Separated Value (CSV)** format. Harry can then copy this and paste it on to any spreadsheet.

Time for action – retrieve CSV data from the chart and update a textarea

1. Create a copy of `SortChartData.html` in the `JavaScriptCapabilities` folder and name it as `RetrieveChartData.html`.

2. Open this new file in a text editor and insert a new button that will appear just beside the button to sort data. The code for the button will be the following:

```
<input type="button" onclick=" fetchData()"
  value="Get Chart Data" />
```

3. After the end of the paragraph element (around line 86) containing the previous button, insert a new line and add the following HTML code:

```
<p>
   <textarea id="CSVData" style="display:none;"
      rows="8" cols="40" readonly="readonly"
      onblur="hideCSVData()"></textarea>
</p>
```

4. Now within the `<head>` of the page, add a new line after the end of the `sortData` function (around line number 48) and insert the following code:

```
function fetchData () {
   var chart = FusionCharts("myChartId"),
      csvData = chart.getCSVData(),
      csvDataArea = document.getElementById("CSVData");
   csvDataArea.innerHTML = csvData;
   csvDataArea.style.display = "block";
   csvDataArea.focus();
}
function hideCSVData () {
   document.getElementById("CSVData").style.display = "none";
}
```

5. Open this HTML file in a browser and when the **Get Chart Data** button is visible, click on it. A textarea will be visible and you will see that the current chart's data is available inside it, as shown in the following screenshot. You can copy this data to the clipboard and paste it in a spreadsheet.

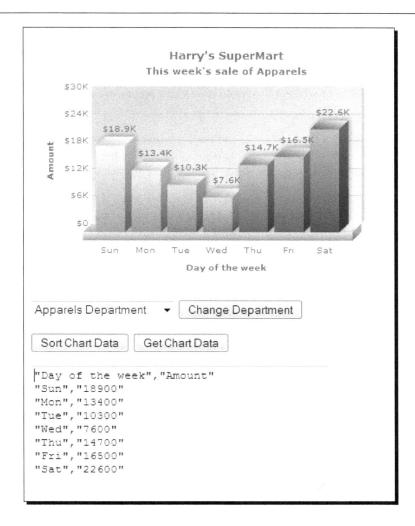

What just happened?

We created a new button and labeled it as **Get Chart Data**. Below this button, we added a `<textarea>` element. This textarea is provided with an ID, `CSVData`, so that we can access it and update the textarea contents with CSV data fetched from the chart. We also set the display style of the textarea to `none`, so that it remains initially hidden.

We created the `fetchData` function to access this textarea and make it visible. After that, we updated its content by fetching the chart's data using the `getDataAsCSV` function.

One can easily configure the separator from a comma to any other character using the chart attribute `exportDataSeparator` of the chart's data XML/JSON. More on configuring the data export options can be found at the **Exporting Chart Data | Using Context Menu** section of the documentation.

We also added some extra tricks to make the textarea read-only, by adding the `readonly="readonly"` attribute to the textarea and setting the cursor focus on the textarea, so that it becomes easier for Harry to copy the data from this.

Once the textarea was made visible, it would appear very odd if it was kept in this state even when the data of the chart changed. Hence, we created a small function called `hideCSVDataArea` to simply hide the textarea by setting the display style back to "none". We added this function to the `onBlur` event of the textarea so that it is called the moment focus shifted to any other item on the page.

If we wanted to fetch data in any other format, we could have simply called `chart.getJSONData()` or `chart.getXMLData()` to get data in JSON or XML formats respectively.

Manipulate chart cosmetics using JavaScript

FusionCharts can be customized in unlimited ways by providing necessary configuration through the data XML (or JSON). The primary configuration options reside as attributes within the `<chart>` tag. These attributes, such as `caption`, `subcaption`, `numberPrefix`, `bgColor`, and many more, are referred to in our realm as **chart attributes**.

Once your chart has been rendered with your customized set of chart attributes, these can be easily modified by using the function `setChartAttribute` of each chart.

For our audit report page, we are going to provide Harry with a subtle feature to hide the data values that are being displayed on every column. With this, he can have an unobstructed view to compare each day's sale.

Time for action – hide data values of the columns

1. Create a copy of `RetrieveChartData.html` in the `JavaScriptCapabilities` folder and name it as `ManipulateCosmetics.html`.

2. Open this file in a text editor and insert another button to appear just beside the button to retrieve chart data as CSV (around line 90). The code for the button will be the following:

```
<input type="button" onclick="updateChartCosmetics()"
  value="Hide Data Values" />
```

3. Now within the `<head>` of the page, add a new line after the end of the `hideCSVData` function (around line number 64) and insert the following code:

```
function updateChartCosmetics () {
  var chart = FusionCharts("myChartId");
  chart.setChartAttribute("showValues", "0");
}
```

4. Open the file in a browser. Once the **Hide Data Values** button is visible, as shown in the following screenshot, click on it and subsequently the values will be hidden:

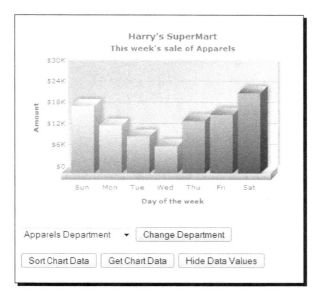

What just happened?

We created a new function called `updateChartCosmetics` to access the chart and set the value of `showValue` chart attribute to `0` by using the `setChartAttribute` function of the chart. This function accepts two parameters, the first being the name of the chart attribute and the second being the new value you want to set for it.

Debugging your charts

Through the course of development of this audit report, if the charts did not render or if you saw a JavaScript error, your best friend at hand would be the debugging capabilities of FusionCharts.

Using the JavaScript debug mode

The JavaScript debug mode helps you display a series of information regarding the chart that might provide you with useful clues to track down errors while rendering your charts.

Time for action – set up the JavaScript debug mode to output in a browser console

1. Create a copy of `ManipulateCosmetics.html` in the `JavaScriptCapabilities` folder and name it as `UsingJSDebugMode.html`.

2. Open this file in a text editor, and within the `<script>` tag we were previously working on, insert the following code:

```
FusionCharts.debugMode.enabled(true);
FusionCharts.debugMode.outputTo(function (message) {
  console.log(message);
});
```

3. Open this HTML file in a browser and open the JavaScript debug console (usually by pressing the *F12* key on your keyboard.) You will see a series of information pertaining to the chart. The following screenshot displays how the console will appear in Google Chrome:

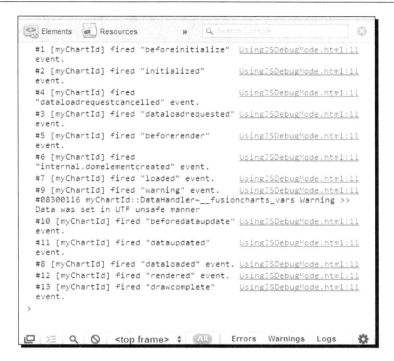

What just happened?

Immediately after including the `FusionCharts.js` script file, we enabled the debug mode using the code `FusionCharts.debugMode.enabled(true)`. This does not start displaying the messages yet. To actually see the message, we specified the message output location by creating a function that logs the output messages to the JavaScript console. We passed this function to the `outputTo` function of the `debugMode` object.

 FusionCharts also provides two simple events called `FC_Error` and `FC_Warning` that are raised when something goes wrong with the chart. These can be used if you need to selectively trap error and warning messages.

Have a go hero

Another way to ease Harry's auditing process is to include *trendines* showing the average sales of the week. This can be done in the same way as we sorted the data. FusionCharts JSON format allows you to introduce trendlines by providing the trendlines as an array. You can find out more about trendlines at the **Quick Chart Configuration** > **Trend Lines & Zones** section of the documentation. To give you a head start, a sample JSON showing a trendline would look similar to the following:

```
{
  "chart": {
    "caption": "Quarterly sale",
    "xaxisname": "Quarters",
    "yaxisname": "Revenue",
    "numberprefix": "$",
  },
  "data": [
    { "label": "Q1", "value": "420000" },
    { "label": "Q2", "value": "660000" },
    { "label": "Q3", "value": "230000" },
    { "label": "Q4", "value": "410000" }
  ],
  "trendlines": [{
    "line": [{
        "startvalue": "600000",
        "valueonright": "1",
        "displayvalue": "Target",
    }]
  }]
}
```

For the audit report, create another button called **View Average Trend** and on the click of the button, execute a function that would calculate the average sale of the week by iterating through the data and then update the data with a trendline object on this value.

 Verify your implementation with the file `GotoHero-DynamicTrendline.html` as a part of the downloadable code samples of this book.

Summary

In this chapter, we developed interactive functionalities around charts using JavaScript.

Using the FusionCharts JavaScript capabilities we:

- Programmatically accessed a chart on a page.
- Developed functionalities around various events raised by the charts.
- Dynamically updated chart data and retrieved data from the chart to provide functionalities involving manipulation of the chart data.
- Programmatically modified chart cosmetics.

We also learned how to track chart errors by using the debug messages.

In our next chapter, we will add drill-down functionality to our charts using various concepts that we have gathered in this chapter.

4
Enabling Drill-down on Charts

Harry is feeling web-savvy and is curious about his website's performance. Today, he wants to review how his online revenues have been growing over the last five years, and, we have been asked to visualize and provide this data in the form of a chart. We can build this chart in two ways.

In the first approach, we can plot a single chart with 60 columns – one column per month for those five years. While this chart lets Harry compare the growth of online revenue month-over-month, it is hard to figure the growth in yearly revenues, as Harry can only see monthly figures and will have to sum up the annual figures mentally – not a mean feat. And doesn't that beat the whole purpose of having a chart in the first place?

The other approach is to first show the yearly revenue of those five years in a column chart. This lets him track the growth of revenue over years. Now, when he needs to see breakdown of a particular year, he can click on the respective year's column in the chart and view monthly data for that year. This approach is better as it first lets him compare the yearly revenue, and then drill-down into the breakdown of a particular year reflecting the monthly revenues. This chapter explains this concept of drill-down in detail.

In this chapter, you will:

- ◆ Learn how to build charts that can drill-down into detailed data
- ◆ Configure the drill-down charts to open in a new window, frame, or pop ups
- ◆ Use JavaScript functions to react to drill-down events
- ◆ Use the LinkedCharts feature of FusionCharts to create multi-level drill-down using a single data source

Before we get on with our first example, let us quickly understand how drill-down works in FusionCharts.

How does drill-down work in FusionCharts?

As we had earlier discussed, the columns, bars, or pie wedges on any chart are called **data plots** of the chart, in FusionCharts parlance. For each such data plot, FusionCharts allows you to define a click event termed as a **link**. This link helps you define drill-down on the chart for each data plot, and can be configured to initiate various actions such as redirecting the browser window to another web page or invoking a JavaScript function present on the page. These actions are collectively termed as **drill-down actions**. We will soon see how to define these links and their corresponding actions.

In order to enable drill-down capabilities on your charts, you need to create two sets of charts—**parent** and **descendant** (or child) charts.

- A **parent chart** is the aggregate chart that the user sees first. This chart contains aggregate data, which upon click leads to the child chart showing the breakdown of data. In the example that we will soon build for Harry, the chart showing the yearly revenue is the parent chart, as Harry can then click on each year to view the monthly breakdown of sales for the specific year.

- A **descendant or child chart** shows the breakdown of the data selected in the parent chart upon clicking. In our example, the charts showing monthly revenue, which are displayed when Harry clicks on a particular year in the parent chart, are the descendant charts.

For our example, we just need to define one level of the **drill-down hierarchy**—from yearly data to monthly data. As such, we need to create one parent chart showing yearly data and five descendant charts representing monthly data, one for each year in the parent chart.

 FusionCharts also allows you to create multi-level drill-down charts with the same ease. Consider an example where you need to first show the data by year, then by quarter, then by month, and finally by day. In this case, the yearly chart is the top most parent chart. The quarterly chart is a descendant of the yearly chart, and parent to the monthly chart. Similarly, the monthly chart is a descendant of the quarterly chart and parent to the daily chart. The daily chart is the only chart that is a sole descendant, without being a parent of any chart.

With this basic know-how in place, let us now build our first chart with drill-down that allows Harry to compare online revenues by year first, and then drill-down into months.

Building our first drill-down chart

We need to create one parent chart and five descendant charts to satisfy Harry's reporting needs. Let us first build the parent chart with drill-down activated for it.

Time for action: building the parent chart

1. Under the `LearningFusionCharts` folder that we had earlier created in *Chapter 1, Introducing FusionCharts*, create a new folder `DrillDown`. This will act as a container for all the examples we will build in this chapter.

2. Copy `FirstChart.html` from the `FirstChart` folder and create a copy in the `DrillDown` folder. Rename it to `YearlyChart.html`.

3. Make the following changes to the code in this file. Essentially, we are changing the chart type to Column 2D, increasing the width to 500 and pointing the URL of the XML data file to `YearlyData.xml`.

```html
<html>
  <body>
    <div id="chartContainer">FusionCharts will load here!</div>
      <script type="text/javascript">
        <!-- var myChart =
          new FusionCharts("../FusionCharts/Column2D.swf",
          "myChartId", "500", "300", "0", "1" );
          myChart.setXMLUrl("YearlyData.xml");
          myChart.render("chartContainer");// -->
      </script>
  </body>
</html>
```

4. Create an XML file in this folder with the name `YearlyData.xml` and type the following data in it:

```
<chart caption='Harry&apos;s SuperMart - Online Revenue'
  subcaption='Last 5 years' xAxisName='Year'
  yAxisName='Amount' numberPrefix='$'>
  <set label='2007' value='145700' link='Monthly2007Chart.html'/>
  <set label='2008' value='180400' link='Monthly2008Chart.html'/>
  <set label='2009' value='345600' link='Monthly2009Chart.html'/>
  <set label='2010' value='567400' link='Monthly2010Chart.html'/>
  <set label='2011' value='856100' link='Monthly2011Chart.html'/>
</chart>
```

5. Open `YearlyChart.html` in your browser. You should see a chart similar to the following screenshot. Try hovering over the columns using your mouse cursor. This is where the magic happens. You will notice that the mouse changes to a hand cursor upon hover, reflecting that a link has been activated for all the columns in this chart. As we have not created the descendant charts page yet, clicking on any of these will lead to *HTTP Error 404 Not Found*.

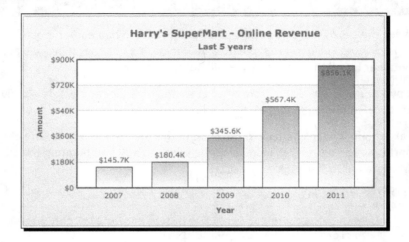

What just happened?

You just created the parent chart and activated the links on each column of the chart by adding the `link` attribute to each `<set>` element.

```
<set label='2007' value='145700' link='Monthly2007Chart.html'/>
```

Each column, when clicked now, will redirect the user to a page containing the descendant chart's page contained as a value of the `link` attribute. In the previous line of XML, we instructed the chart to redirect the browser to `Monthly2007Chart.html` whenever Harry clicks on the column for `2007`. Similarly, for other years, we have defined a link attribute and pointed it to a page containing its descendant chart, which we will build next.

Time for action – building the descendant chart

1. Create `Monthly2007Chart.html` in the `DrillDown` folder and type the following code in it.

```
<html>
  <head>
    <title>Online Revenue - For 2007</title>
    <script type="text/javascript"
      src="../FusionCharts/FusionCharts.js">
```

```
        </script>
      </head>
      <body>
        <div id="chartContainer">FusionCharts will load here!</div>
        <script type="text/javascript">
          <!-- var myChart =
            new FusionCharts("../FusionCharts/Column2D.swf",
            "myChartId", "500", "300", "0", "1" );
            myChart.setXMLUrl("Monthly2007Data.xml");
            myChart.render("chartContainer"); // -->
        </script>
        <a href='YearlyChart.html'>&lt;&lt; Back to yearly chart</a>
      </body>
    </html>
```

2. Create an XML file named `Monthly2007Data.xml` in the same folder, type in the following XML representing the monthly breakdown of online revenues for 2011:

```
<chart caption='Harry&apos;s SuperMart - Monthly online revenue'
  subcaption='For 2007' xAxisName='Month' yAxisName='Amount'
  numberPrefix='$' rotateValues='1'>
  <set label='Jan' value='9325'/>
  <set label='Feb' value='10928'/>
  <set label='Mar' value='10199'/>
  <set label='Apr' value='11656'/>
  <set label='May' value='12822'/>
  <set label='Jun' value='10199'/>
  <set label='Jul' value='13259'/>
  <set label='Aug' value='8742'/>
  <set label='Sep' value='18941'/>
  <set label='Oct' value='14570'/>
  <set label='Nov' value='11656'/>
  <set label='Dec' value='13404'/>
</chart>
```

3. Repeat steps 1 and 2 to create HTML and XML files for the years 2008, 2009, 2010 and 2011. The format that we have used for naming the HTML file is `Monthly{yyyy}Chart.html` and that for XML is `Monthly{yyyy}Data.html`, where {yyyy} is to be replaced by the actual year. For the sake of brevity, we are not repeating the data of each year here. However, the entire code is available as part of the download materials of this book.

4. Open `YearlyChart.html` in your browser and click on the column for the year 2011. You will be redirected to `Monthly2011Chart.html` that contains the descendant chart containing the monthly breakdown of revenue for 2011, as shown in the following screenshot:

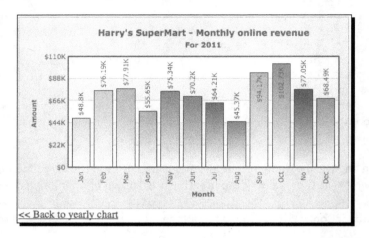

Bingo! This achieves exactly what we had set out to do.

What just happened?

You just created a dashboard-like application for Harry that lets him view the revenue by year and then drill-down into any year to see the monthly breakdown.

Here is what happened behind the scenes. When you add the `link` attribute for any `<set>` element with its value as a URL, FusionCharts activates the link for that data plot. Now, whenever the data plot is clicked, FusionCharts redirects the browser to the defined URL. So, when you clicked on the column for 2011, the chart redirected you to `Monthly2011Chart.html`, which contained the descendant chart for 2011.

Each descendant chart, in this example, has an HTML page of its own, containing the chart with the monthly breakdown for that year, along with a link to go back to the parent chart.

Cool, isn't it? Let us now explore some configurations that let you open the descendant chart in a new window, pop-ups, and frames.

Opening descendant charts in a new window

In this example, all the descendant charts opened in the same window, thereby replacing the parent chart. However, you can instruct FusionCharts to open the descendant charts in a new window by appending the prefix n- before the link. Following is an example of such an XML, where each link, upon clicking, opens the descendant chart in a new window:

```
<chart caption='Harry&apos;s SuperMart - Online Revenue'
  subcaption='Last 5 years' xAxisName='Year' yAxisName='Amount'
  numberPrefix='$'>
  <set label='2007' value='145700' link='n-Monthly2007Chart.html'/>
  <set label='2008' value='180400' link='n-Monthly2008Chart.html'/>
  <set label='2009' value='345600' link='n-Monthly2009Chart.html'/>
  <set label='2010' value='567400' link='n-Monthly2010Chart.html'/>
  <set label='2011' value='856100' link='n-Monthly2011Chart.html'/>
</chart>
```

This method is useful when you want to retain the parent chart upon clicking, but at the same time, load the child chart separately.

Opening descendant charts in a pop-up window

You can also open the descendant charts in a pop-up window, instead of a new window. To do this, the following format for the link attribute has to be used:

```
<set … link='p-windowName,attribute1=value1,attribute2=value2-
  descendant_chart.html' />
```

Note the p- prefix before each link indicates that the link has to be opened in a pop-up window. It is followed by windowName, which is a unique name given to each pop-up window. If you want all the descendant charts to open in the same pop-up window, provide a common windowName across all <set> elements in an XML file.

Additionally, for the pop-up window, you can specify a bunch of attributes such as width, height, resizable, scrollbars, menubar, toolbar, and location. These are provided as a comma-separated list, as in the following XML:

```
<chart caption='Harry&apos;s SuperMart - Online Revenue'
  subcaption='Last 5 years' xAxisName='Year' yAxisName='Amount'
  numberPrefix='$'>
  <set label='2007' value='145700' link='p-
    window1,width=550,height=340,toolbar=no,scrollbars=no,
    resizable=no-Monthly2007Chart.html'/>
  <set label='2008' value='180400' link='p-
    window2,width=550,height=340,toolbar=no,scrollbars=no,
    resizable=no-Monthly2008Chart.html'/>
  <set label='2009' value='345600' link='p-
    window3,width=550,height=340,toolbar=no,scrollbars=no,
```

```
        resizable=no-Monthly2009Chart.html'/>
    <set label='2010' value='567400' link='p-
        window4,width=550,height=340,toolbar=no,scrollbars=no,
        resizable=no-Monthly2010Chart.html'/>
    <set label='2011' value='856100' link='p-
        window5,width=550,height=340,toolbar=no,scrollbars=no,
        resizable=no-Monthly2011Chart.html'/>
</chart>
```

In this XML, we have provided a name to each window, thereby resulting in each descendant chart opening a window of its own.

Opening descendant charts in a frame

If you have a web page with frames, FusionCharts allows you to load the parent chart in one frame, and open the descendant charts in another frame. This is made possible by the following configuration in XML:

```
<set ... link='f-FrameName-descendant_chart.html' ... >
```

Note the `f-` prefix before the link. It indicates that the link has to be opened in a frame. Next, you need to provide the `FrameName` attribute which points to the frame that would actually contain the descendent chart. For example, if we had a frame with the name `childFrame`, our XML would look similar to the following for each descendent chart to load in this frame:

```
<chart caption='Harry&apos;s SuperMart - Online Revenue'
    subcaption='Last 5 years' xAxisName='Year' yAxisName='Amount'
    numberPrefix='$'>
    <set label='2007' value='145700' link='f-childFrame-
        Monthly2007Chart.html'/>
    <set label='2008' value='180400' link='f-childFrame-
        Monthly2008Chart.html'/>
    <set label='2009' value='345600' link='f-childFrame-
        Monthly2009Chart.html'/>
    <set label='2010' value='567400' link='f-childFrame-
        Monthly2010Chart.html'/>
    <set label='2011' value='856100' link='f-childFrame-
        Monthly2011Chart.html'/>
</chart>
```

Invoking JavaScript functions on a link click event

FusionCharts also allows you to invoke JavaScript functions instead of opening another web page, when the link on a chart is clicked. This opens a wide variety of possibilities. For example, upon the click of a column, you can track its ID and show additional information relevant to the column in a JavaScript lightbox or equivalent. Or, you may update multiple other charts present on the same page, based on this selection. The possibilities are endless.

The format for specifying a JavaScript link is as follows:

```
<set ... link="j-javaScriptFunction-parameter1,parameter2"/>
```

Here, the `j-` prefix instructs the chart that a JavaScript function named `javaScriptFunction` has to be invoked when the data plot belonging to this `<set>` element is clicked. Also, a comma-separated list of parameters after the second hyphen gets passed to this function. In JavaScript parlance, this is equivalent to invoking the following JavaScript code:

```
javaScriptFunction("parameter1,parameter2");
```

`javaScriptFunction` is a custom function that needs to be defined by you in the page containing the chart, within the same scope.

If we had to build a drill-down example, which invokes a JavaScript function to alert the label and value of the column clicked, the XML would need to be modified to:

```
<chart caption='Harry&apos;s SuperMart - Online Revenue'
  subcaption='Last 5 years' xAxisName='Year' yAxisName='Amount'
  numberPrefix='$'>
  <set label='2007' value='145700' link='j-myJS-2007,145700'/>
  <set label='2008' value='180400' link='j-myJS-2008,180400'/>
  <set label='2009' value='345600' link='j-myJS-2009,345600'/>
  <set label='2010' value='567400' link='j-myJS-2010,567400'/>
  <set label='2011' value='856100' link='j-myJS-2011,856100'/>
</chart>
```

Here, we are instructing the chart to call the `myJS` JavaScript function when each column is clicked. Also, for each column, we are passing its label and value as a single string combined using a comma, for example, `2007,145700`.

The HTML page containing the chart would need to define this `myJS` function. In a simple implementation, as the following, we are just requesting the parameter to be passed to the function, splitting the comma-separated parameters, comprising of label and value, into an array using JavaScript's split function, and finally showing it in a message box:

```
<html>
  <head>
    <title>Online Revenue - Last 5 years</title>
    <script type="text/javascript"
      src="../FusionCharts/FusionCharts.js">
    </script>
    <SCRIPT LANGUAGE="JavaScript">
      <!-- function myJS(myVar){//Split comma separated parameter
        comprising of label and value into array. var params =
        myVar.split(",");alert("Label: " + params[0] + " and Value: "
        + params[1])} //-->
```

```
      </SCRIPT>
    </head>
    <body>
      <div id="chartContainer">FusionCharts will load here!</div>
      <script type="text/javascript">
        <!-- var myChart =
          new FusionCharts("../FusionCharts/Column2D.swf",
          "myChartId", "500", "300", "0", "1" );
          myChart.setXMLUrl("YearlyChartJavaScript.xml");
          myChart.render("chartContainer");// -->
      </script>
    </body>
  </html>
```

When you run this example, and click on a column, you should get a JavaScript alert with the label and value of the column, as shown in the following screenshot:

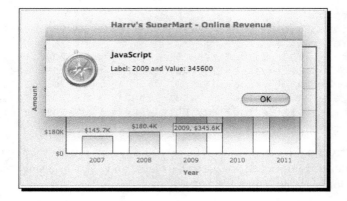

With this example, we have covered all the basic drill-down functionalities offered by FusionCharts. You learned how to activate drill-down to a chart, open the links in the same window, new window, pop-ups, frames, and even invoke JavaScript functions. By using these methods, you can now easily build multi-level dashboards that are detailed and interactive. The crux of a building engaging drill-down reporting is how you split the data. It should be on meaningful parameters such as aggregation or date/time. An example of aggregation is when you drill-down from continents to countries to regions to cities, and so on. And, we have already seen how to create drill-down on date/time.

Let us now explore a new concept that helps you cut down your effort in building drill-down charts—**LinkedCharts**.

LinkedCharts for simplified drill-downs

In our earlier example, we had to create one web page for each descendant chart. This could mean that if you have dozens of data points in your parent chart, you will need to create dozens of HTML pages, each to contain a descendant chart. This could get murky and unmanageable.

In an effort to curtail this, FusionCharts has a nifty feature called LinkedCharts. Using LinkedCharts, you can do one of the following:

1. Reduce the number of web pages to just one by curtailing the creation of all web pages that contain descendant charts. This web page contains the parent chart and loads the descendant charts in this page itself, as and when required. However, the number of XML files in this case remains the same, one for the parent chart, and one for each descendant chart.

2. Or, you can even go further and curtail all the XML files of descendant charts. In this case, all the data is contained in the XML of the parent chart.

Let us consider an example for both these scenarios. First, we will see how to eliminate the creation of web pages for descendant charts.

Time for action – using LinkedCharts to eliminate multiple web pages for descendant charts

1. Create a copy of `YearlyChart.html` from the previous example and rename it as `LinkedChart.html`. Change the URL of the XML data file to `LinkedChartData.xml`.

2. Create an XML file in this folder with the name `LinkedChartData.xml` and type the following data in it:

```
<chart caption='Harry&apos;s SuperMart - Online Revenue'
  subcaption='Last 5 years'
  xAxisName='Year' yAxisName='Amount' numberPrefix='$'>
  <set label='2007' value='145700' link='newchart-xmlurl-
    Monthly2007Data.xml'/>
  <set label='2008' value='180400' link='newchart-xmlurl-
    Monthly2008Data.xml'/>
  <set label='2009' value='345600' link='newchart-xmlurl-
    Monthly2009Data.xml'/>
  <set label='2010' value='567400' link='newchart-xmlurl-
    Monthly2010Data.xml'/>
  <set label='2011' value='856100' link='newchart-xmlurl-
    Monthly2011Data.xml'/>
</chart>
```

3. Open `LinkedChart.html` in your browser. You will first see the yearly revenue chart showing data for the last five years, as we have seen earlier.

4. Now, click on any of the columns. Here is where the magic happens. You will see a descendant chart showing data with the monthly breakdown for that year. However, in this chart, you will also find a **Back** button at the top-right corner, which when clicked, takes you back to the parent chart, without changing the web page. This is the magic of **LinkedCharts**.

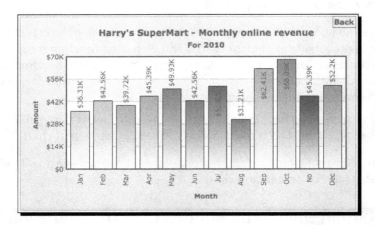

Let us understand how this magic happened.

What just happened?

Like before, we created a chart and defined the `link` attribute for each `<set>` element, which activated the links for the data plot. However, this time, the links defined are different. They are prefixed with `newchart-` and are defined as in the following line of code:

```
<set label='2007' value='145700' link='newchart-xmlurl-
   Monthly2007Data.xml'/>
```

Here, `newchart` is a keyword that instructs FusionCharts' JavaScript class to replace the parent chart with a new chart, with data from `Monthly2007Data.xml`. The keyword `xmlurl` indicates that the data for the new chart has been provided as a URL to the XML file, followed by the relative path of the XML data file for the child chart.

Each column, when clicked now, creates a new chart by loading the data from the specified XML file and replaces the original chart. The new chart also provides a **Back** button, which when clicked, removes the descendant chart and renders the parent chart again. The FusionCharts' JavaScript class keeps track of all this in the background and manages it for you, without you having to code anything extra. Super cool, isn't it?

Next, let us explore the alternate way to build **LinkedCharts** where we condense all the XML files into a single file.

Time for action – creating LinkedCharts using a single XML source

1. Create a copy of `LinkedChart.html` and name it as `LinkedChartSingleSource.html`. Change the URL of the XML data file to `LinkedChartSingleSourceData.xml`.

2. Create an XML file in this folder with the name `LinkedChartSingleSourceData.xml` and type the following data in it:

```
<chart caption='Harry&apos;s SuperMart - Online Revenue'
  subcaption='Last 5 years' xAxisName='Year' yAxisName='Amount'
  numberPrefix='$'>
  <set label='2007' value='145700' link='newchart-xml-
    monthly2007'/>
  <set label='2008' value='180400' link='newchart-xml-
    monthly2008'/>
  <set label='2009' value='345600' link='newchart-xml-
    monthly2009'/>
  <set label='2010' value='567400' link='newchart-xml-
    monthly2010'/>
  <set label='2011' value='856100' link='newchart-xml-
    monthly2011'/>
  <linkeddata id="monthly2007">
    <chart caption='Harry&apos;s SuperMart - Monthly online
      revenue' subcaption='For 2007' xAxisName='Month'
      yAxisName='Amount' numberPrefix='$' rotateValues='1'>
      <set label='Jan' value='9325'/>
      <set label='Feb' value='10928'/>
      <set label='Mar' value='10199'/>
      <set label='Apr' value='11656'/>
      <set label='May' value='12822'/>
      <set label='Jun' value='10199'/>
      <set label='Jul' value='13259'/>
      <set label='Aug' value='8742'/>
      <set label='Sep' value='18941'/>
      <set label='Oct' value='14570'/>
      <set label='Nov' value='11656'/>
      <set label='Dec' value='13404'/>
    </chart>
  </linkeddata>
  <linkeddata id="monthly2008">
```

```
  <chart caption='Harry&apos;s SuperMart - Monthly online
    revenue' subcaption='For 2008' xAxisName='Month'
    yAxisName='Amount' numberPrefix='$' rotateValues='1'>
    <set label='Jan' value='11546'/>
    <set label='Feb' value='13530'/>
    <set label='Mar' value='12628'/>
    <set label='Apr' value='14432'/>
    <set label='May' value='15875'/>
    <set label='Jun' value='12628'/>
    <set label='Jul' value='16416'/>
    <set label='Aug' value='10824'/>
    <set label='Sep' value='23452'/>
    <set label='Oct' value='18040'/>
    <set label='Nov' value='14432'/>
    <set label='Dec' value='16597'/>
  </chart>
</linkeddata>
<linkeddata id="monthly2009">
  <chart caption='Harry&apos;s SuperMart - Monthly online
    revenue' subcaption='For 2009' xAxisName='Month'
    yAxisName='Amount' numberPrefix='$' rotateValues='1'>
    <set label='Jan' value='22118'/>
    <set label='Feb' value='25920'/>
    <set label='Mar' value='24192'/>
    <set label='Apr' value='27648'/>
    <set label='May' value='30413'/>
    <set label='Jun' value='25920'/>
    <set label='Jul' value='31450'/>
    <set label='Aug' value='19008'/>
    <set label='Sep' value='38016'/>
    <set label='Oct' value='41472'/>
    <set label='Nov' value='27648'/>
    <set label='Dec' value='31795'/>
  </chart>
</linkeddata>
<linkeddata id="monthly2010">
  <chart caption='Harry&apos;s SuperMart - Monthly online
    revenue' subcaption='For 2010' xAxisName='Month'
    yAxisName='Amount' numberPrefix='$' rotateValues='1'>
    <set label='Jan' value='36314'/>
```

```
            <set label='Feb' value='42555'/>
            <set label='Mar' value='39718'/>
            <set label='Apr' value='45392'/>
            <set label='May' value='49931'/>
            <set label='Jun' value='42555'/>
            <set label='Jul' value='51633'/>
            <set label='Aug' value='31207'/>
            <set label='Sep' value='62414'/>
            <set label='Oct' value='68088'/>
            <set label='Nov' value='45392'/>
            <set label='Dec' value='52201'/>
        </chart>
    </linkeddata>
    <linkeddata id="monthly2011">
        <chart caption='Harry&apos;s SuperMart - Monthly online
            revenue' subcaption='For 2011' xAxisName='Month'
            yAxisName='Amount' numberPrefix='$' rotateValues='1'>
            <set label='Jan' value='48798'/>
            <set label='Feb' value='76193'/>
            <set label='Mar' value='77905'/>
            <set label='Apr' value='55647'/>
            <set label='May' value='75337'/>
            <set label='Jun' value='70200'/>
            <set label='Jul' value='64208'/>
            <set label='Aug' value='45373'/>
            <set label='Sep' value='94171'/>
            <set label='Oct' value='102732'/>
            <set label='Nov' value='77049'/>
            <set label='Dec' value='68488'/>
        </chart>
    </linkeddata>
</chart>
```

3. Open `LinkedChartSingleSource.html` in your browser. You will first see the yearly revenue chart showing data for the last five years. Click on any of the columns. As seen earlier, you will again see a descendant chart showing data with monthly breakdown for that year, with the **Back** button at the top-right corner, which when clicked, takes you back to the parent chart, without changing the web page.

What just happened?

What has changed in this example, compared to the previous **LinkedCharts**, is that the entire drill-down is driven through a single datasource, `LinkedChartSingleSourceData.xml`.

Like the other chart we created using **LinkedCharts**, in this chart also we provided the `link` for each `<set>` element with the `newchart-` keyword. However, unlike earlier, in this XML, we do not point to external XML files for each descendant chart, which was earlier provided after the `xmlurl` keyword. Instead, here we are embedding the XML of each descendant chart within the parent XML file itself, and giving it a unique identifier, as in the following for the year 2007:

```
<linkeddata id="monthly2007">
  <chart caption='Harry&apos;s SuperMart - Monthly online revenue'
    subcaption='For 2007' xAxisName='Month' yAxisName='Amount'
    numberPrefix='$' rotateValues='1'>
    <set label='Jan' value='9325'/>
    <set label='Feb' value='10928'/>
    <set label='Mar' value='10199'/>
    <set label='Apr' value='11656'/>
    <set label='May' value='12822'/>
    <set label='Jun' value='10199'/>
    <set label='Jul' value='13259'/>
    <set label='Aug' value='8742'/>
    <set label='Sep' value='18941'/>
    <set label='Oct' value='14570'/>
    <set label='Nov' value='11656'/>
    <set label='Dec' value='13404'/>
  </chart>
</linkeddata>
```

In the previous code, we have created a `<linkeddata>` element that contains the entire XML data for the chart representing the monthly data for 2007. We have assigned it a unique string identifier `monthly2007`, that has been provided as a value for the `id` attribute of the `<linkeddata>` element. It is by using this unique identifier that you map the descendent chart's XML data to the parent chart's data plot, as in the following XML code:

```
<set label='2007' value='145700' link='newchart-xml-monthly2007'/>
```

Here, we are telling FusionCharts to create a new chart by reading embedded data whose unique identifier is `monthly2007`, when the column for 2007 is clicked in the parent chart. Note how we are using the `xml` keyword after `newchart` to indicate the embedded data to FusionCharts, as opposed to the `xmlurl` keyword, that instructs FusionCharts to load an external XML file.

And with this method, you have converted one parent chart XML file and five descendant charts' XML into a single XML source. However, we do not recommend this method when you have large datasets, as condensing all of the data into a single datasource increases the size of the XML file and therefore the initial load time for the chart also increases.

Summary

In this chapter, we learned how to create drill-down charts using FusionCharts that help you build engaging and interactive dashboards or reports.

Specifically, we covered:

- ◆ How easy it is to create charts that can be clicked to show detailed data
- ◆ How to configure the child chart to show in a new window, pop-ups, and frames
- ◆ How to invoke JavaScript functions when a data plot on the chart is clicked
- ◆ Finally, we used the LinkedCharts feature of FusionCharts that simplifies building multi-level drill-down charts

Now that we have learned how to build charts, customize them, integrate them with JavaScript, and add drill-down to them, let us explore how to allow the export of charts as images and data as CSV, which is the topic of the next chapter.

5
Exporting Charts

The quick audit process that we had earlier setup for Harry's SuperMart had been a great success. Consequently, Harry now wants to share the reports with his marketing managers. Quite naturally, Harry feels that sending the reports over e-mail will be the easiest process. Fortunately, FusionCharts provides us with the ability to export charts as images and PDF documents. In this chapter, we will learn how to export our charts so that we can develop features around them.

At a glance, we will learn how to:

- Save a chart as an image or PDF document from within the browser and onto your computer.
- Customize various export related configurations such as the export file format, file name and others.
- Use JavaScript to export charts.
- Save the chart as an image to a remote server.

A word on how the export process works

The charts can be exported in three different formats, JPEG image, PNG image, and PDF document. Furthermore, the charts can either be exported locally at client-side or be sent to a server to be processed, or saved there. Upon initiation of the export process, the chart captures its own image in bitmap format. This bitmap image is passed on to an export component for further processing.

When exporting at client-side, the charts need to be assisted by an export component SWF to process and save the file. Charts exported at client-side add no additional load on the server. This is extremely beneficial when there are too many people exporting charts at the same time.

On the other hand, for server-side export, the exported image from the chart is processed by a server-side export component script. With this feature, the charts can be processed by the server or be saved as an image on the server for later use or for archival purposes.

Export charts at client-side

Enabling charts to export at client side involves a two-step process. First, we need to configure individual charts' export attributes and then we need to include an additional component for saving the exported charts. This additional component is called the **FusionCharts Export Component**. It is an SWF file, shipped as `FCExporter.swf`, whose work is to process the exported charts and display additional controls such as buttons to save the exported chart.

 The export component SWF file uses the additional benefits of ActionScript 3.0 to process the exported charts and consequently requires a minimum of the Flash Player version 10 plugin to be available.

You will also require an additional JavaScript file, `FusionChartsExportComponent.js`, which is available within the downloadable package inside the `Charts` folder, beside the `FusionCharts.js` file. This file allows the charts and the export component SWF to communicate with each other.

Time for action – enable exporting of charts using the context menu

1. Under the `LearningFusionCharts` folder that we have been using all along, create a new folder named `ExportingCharts`. We will use this folder to store our files as we proceed in this chapter.

2. Within this new folder, create a new file `ExportUsingContextMenu.html` and type the following contents into it:

```
<html>
  <head>
    <title>Audit Report of Harry&apos;s SuperMart</title>
    <script type="text/javascript"
      src="../FusionCharts/FusionCharts.js">
```

```
    </script>
    <script type="text/javascript"
      src="../FusionCharts/FusionChartsExportComponent.js">
    </script>
    <script type="text/javascript"><!--
      var chartObj =
      new FusionCharts("../FusionCharts/Column3D.swf",
      "salesChart", "400","300"),
      exportComponentObj =
        new FusionChartsExportObject("exportComponent",
        "../FusionCharts/FCExporter.swf");
      function loadReport () {
        chartObj.setXMLUrl("ApparelSale_ExportEnabled.xml");
        chartObj.render("chartContainer");
        exportComponentObj.Render("exporterContainer");
      }
    // -->
    </script>
  </head>
  <body onload="loadReport()">
    <div id="chartContainer">FusionCharts will load here!</div>
    <div id="exporterContainer"></div>
  </body>
</html>
```

3. Beside this newly created HTML file, create a new XML file called `ApparelSale_ExportEnabled.xml` that will serve as the chart's datasource. Type the following lines of code into it:

```
<chart caption="Harry&apos;s SuperMart"
  subcaption="This week&apos;s sale of Apparels"
  xAxisName="Day of the week"  yAxisName="Amount"
  numberPrefix="$"
  exportEnabled="1"
  exportAtClient="1"
  exportHandler="exportComponent"
  exportFileName="SuperMart Report"
  exportFormats="PNG=Export chart as Image|PDF=Export chart as
    PDF" exportDialogMessage="Exporting Report: ">
  <set label="Sun" value="18900" />
  <set label="Mon" value="13400" />
  <set label="Tue" value="10300" />
  <set label="Wed" value="7600" />
  <set label="Thu" value="14700" />
  <set label="Fri" value="16500" />
  <set label="Sat" value="22600" />
</chart>
```

4. Open the HTML file in your favorite browser. Once the chart has fully rendered itself, right-click anywhere on the chart to show the chart's context-menu. On the menu, select the **Export chart as Image** option, as shown in the following screenshot:

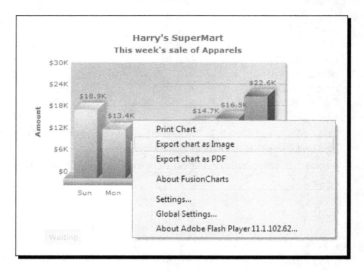

5. A progress bar is displayed overlaying the chart. This indicates how much of the exporting process is complete, as shown in the following screenshot. Wait for this process to complete.

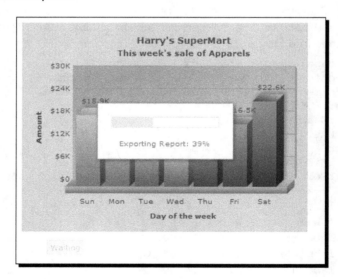

6. Once the progress bar disappears, you will notice the disabled **Waiting** button now getting enabled and being renamed to **Save**, as shown in the following screenshot. Click on this button and save the file within a folder of your choice.

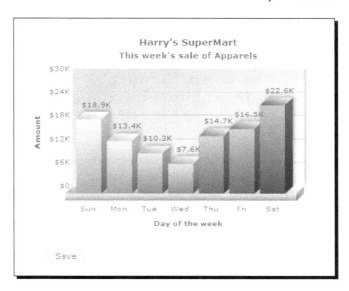

7. Open the folder where you have saved the exported chart and open the file to see the results.

What just happened?

We started by creating an HTML page to render a single chart in the same way we created them in earlier chapters. Additionally, we had to render the export component, for which we included a second JavaScript file called `FusionChartsExportComponent.js` right after the inclusion of the `FusionCharts.js` file.

The line of code `exportComponentObj = new FusionChartsExportObject("exp ortComponent", "../FusionCharts/FCExporter.swf");` instantiated the export component with the ID `exportComponent`. Then, right after the chart's container HTML `<div>` element, we added another `<div>` element with the ID `exporterContainer`. On loading the page, alongside the chart, we also rendered the export component by calling the `Render` function on the export component JavaScript object. As a parameter to the `Render` function, we passed on the ID, `exporterContainer`, of the HTML `<div>` element where we want the export component to render. Once rendered, the export component sits in the *waiting* state until it receives the exported image data from a chart.

We have linked the chart and the export component by configuring the data XML of the chart. The minimal configuration that is needed to set up exporting capabilities consists of three chart attributes:

Attribute	Purpose
`exportEnabled`	This instructs the chart to enable the chart's exporting capabilities. For the chart to respond to any export related functionalities, the value of this needs to be set to `1`.
`exportAtClient`	When this is set to `1`, the chart forwards the exported data to an export component on the page. Otherwise, the chart posts the data to a server.
`exportHandler`	This attribute helps the chart to identify the export component to which it should send the exported data. The value of this attribute should be equal to the ID of the export component to which you want the chart data to be exported. In case the chart is configured to export to a server, the value of this attribute should be the URL of the server-side export component.
	For our audit report we set our export component's ID as `exportComponent`, and thus set the value of the `exportHandler` attribute to the same as the ID.

There are more than a dozen other export related configurations available and we have taken the liberty of using the following to further customize our chart:

Attribute	Purpose
`exportFileName`	We configured the filename that will be displayed when one tries to save the chart. The default is `FusionCharts` and we changed that to `SuperMart Report`.
`exportFormats`	FusionCharts provides two image formats to export your chart, JPEG and PNG. It also allows you to export charts as PDF documents.
	For our audit report, we decided to drop JPEG and retain only PNG and PDF. The value of this attribute should provide the list of export formats separated by the pipe (|) symbol. For each format name, you can even customize the text to be displayed on the context menu by specifying it after the format name with an equals (=) sign.
	We set the value to `PNG=Export chart as Image|PDF=Export chart as PDF`.
`exportDialogMessage`	This allows us to configure the message that is displayed while the chart shows the progress percentage of export. We configured this to further personalize the report page.

For more export related configurations, refer to the **Exporting Charts as PDF/Images | XML Attributes** section of FusionCharts documentation.

Finally, when this page is loaded within a browser, the export component shows a disabled button in waiting state. Once the chart has completed capturing its bitmap data, it forwards this to the export component and this button gets enabled. The button's label changes from **Waiting** to **Save** and allows users to click on it. When clicked, the file save dialog box opens and the exported chart can be saved as an image or a PDF file (depending upon which format it was exported in.)

Pop quiz – know the possibilities

1. What are the formats in which charts can be exported?

2. Exporting charts at client-side requires you to add what additional items to the page?

    a. Include an additional JavaScript file called `FusionChartsExportComponent.js`

    b. Render an additional SWF called `FCExporter.swf`

    c. Both of these

3. What are the basic XML/JSON chart attributes required to enable the client-side exporting capabilities of a chart?

Customizing the export component

Now that we have the basic exporting process ready, we will concentrate on visually customizing the export component, resizing its buttons and changing the button label.

Time for action – customize the export component attributes

1. Duplicate the previously created `ExportUsingContextMenu.html` and save as `CustomizeClientSideExport.html`.

2. Open the `CustomizeClientSideExport.html` file within a text editor of your choice, and replace the export component instantiation code (lines 13 to 14) with the following updated code, essentially passing a third parameter for customizing various aspects of the export component:

```
exportComponentObj =
  new FusionChartsExportObject("exportComponent",
  "../FusionCharts/FCExporter.swf", {
    btnSaveTitle: "Save Report",
    width: "130",
```

```
          height: "22",
          btnWidth: "100",
          btnHeight: "22",
          vMargin: "0"
   });
```

3. Within the `loadReport` function, (at around line 26) delete the line `exportComponentObj.Render("exporterContainer");`.This prevents the export component from rendering along with the chart. There is a good reason for doing this and we will look into this down the line.

4. After the end of the `loadReport` function (around line 27), insert a new line and add the following lines of code:

```
chartObj.addEventListener("exportReady", function () {
  exportComponentObj.Render("exporterContainer");
});
```

5. Open `CustomizeClientSideExport.html` within a browser of your choice and wait for the chart to render. Note that the **Waiting** button is no longer visible. Now, right-click on the chart and select the context menu item **Export chart as Image**.

6. Once the capturing progress bar disappears, the export component should be visible as a **Save Report** button, as shown in the following screenshot. Click on this button and save the file within a folder of your choice.

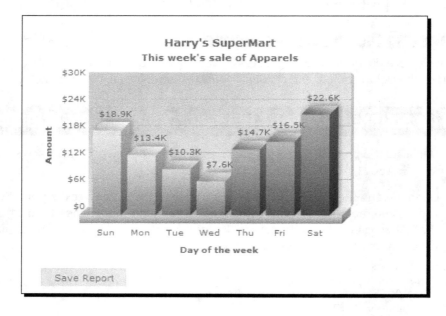

What just happened?

The export component was customized by sending a third (but optional) parameter to the export component constructor. The third parameter accepts an object with the export component configurations as a key-value pair.

 One can also configure the component attributes even after instantiation, by updating the properties of the componentAttributes object of the JavaScript instance of the export component. For example, if your export component's JavaScript instance name is exportComponentObj and you want to set the attribute defaultExportFormat to PDF, then your code would be exportComponentObj.componentAttributes. defaultExportFormat = "PDF";.

The export component accepts many attributes to configure its behavior and user interface. For the audit report, we have used just six of them, as mentioned in the following table:

Component Attribute	Purpose
btnSaveTitle	We have configured the label of the button to show as **Save Report** when the export component is visible. The default label is simply **Save**.
width	The width of the export component is adjusted to match the increased width of the updated button label.
height	The height of the export component is adjusted to match the increased height of the updated button label.
btnWidth	The width of the export component's **Save** button is adjusted to match the increased width of the updated button label.
btnHeight	The height of the export component's **Save** button is adjusted to match the height of the button to the rest of the buttons.
vMargin	This attribute sets the distance at which the export component's button and other UI elements are shown from the top.
	We set it to 0 because we do not need any extra space (margin) on top of the button.

For the complete list of component attributes, refer to the **Exporting Charts as PDF or Images | JavaScript Reference | Component Attributes** section of FusionCharts documentation.

Next, we decided to not show the *Waiting* state of the export component. For this, we simply did not render the export component until the chart had completed exporting itself. We deleted the line `exportComponentObj.Render("exporterContainer");` and created a new event listener for the `exportReady` event of the chart. Within this new event listener, we added the code to render the export component. The `exportReady` event of the chart is fired immediately after the chart has completed exporting its image.

> The export component can be further customized to add UI elements such as an export format chooser and also to allow exporting of multiple charts by setting its *display mode*. The documentation section **Exporting Charts as PDF or Images | Client-side Export | Component UI** explains this in details.
>
> The export component can also be configured to perform batch export of multiple charts on a page. It can act as a single UI element that is able to manage multiple charts exporting its data to it. The exported charts can be individually saved or be combined and saved as a single file. More on this is explained within the **Exporting Charts as PDF or Images | Batch Exporting Charts** section of the documentation.

With this, we completed adding the feature of exporting and saving the charts as image and PDF documents at client-side. Next up, we will look into the ability of FusionCharts to send the exported charts to the server. But before that, we will take a look at how the export process can be controlled using JavaScript. That will allow us to easily implement both server-side and client-side export processes on the same chart.

Export charts using JavaScript API

Instead of Harry having to always right-click on the chart and then select export options, it would be easier if we had buttons below the chart that could export the chart on a single click. To implement this, we need to utilize the export related JavaScript functions of the chart.

Time for action – create a button to export the chart

1. Create a copy of `CustomizeClientSideExport.html` and save it as `ExportUsingJavaScriptAPI.html`.

2. Open this new HTML file using a text editor and locate the `<script>` within the HTML `<head>` element within which we have written our previous set of code. At the end of the script block (around line 31), insert a new line and type the following lines of code:

```
function beginChartExport () {
  if(chartObj.hasRendered && chartObj.hasRendered()) {
    chartObj.exportChart();
  }
  else {
    alert("Please wait for the chart to render.");
  }
}
```

3. Locate the export component container `<div>` HTML element with ID `exporterContainer` (around line 47) and add the following HTML code containing the button to initiate the chart export:

```
<p id="exportControls">
  <input type="button" value="Export Chart"
    onclick="beginChartExport()" />
</p>
```

4. Now open the `ExportUsingJavaScriptAPI.html` file within a browser and click on the newly added button labeled **Export Chart** as shown in the following screenshot:

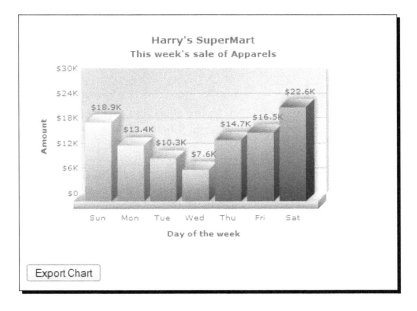

5. On clicking the button, the chart will begin its export process in a similar fashion, as happened when initiated using the context menu. Wait for this process to complete.

6. Once the export process is complete, the export component's **Save Report** button will be visible as shown in the following screenshot. Click on this button and you will notice the chart is ready to be saved as a PNG image.

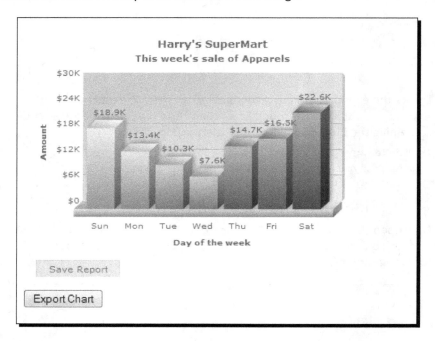

What just happened?

Instead of asking Harry to always right-click on the chart and then select export options, we added an HTML button to execute a JavaScript function to initiate the export process of the chart.

Every FusionCharts JavaScript instance object has a function called `exportChart` that can initiate the export process. For our audit report page, we created a function called `beginChartExport` that checked whether the chart had completely rendered or not, and then initiated export on it. It is important that the export is initiated only after the chart has completely rendered itself. Otherwise, you may end up exporting a partially rendered chart during its animation stage. The code `chartObj.hasRendered()` helps to determine whether the chart has fully rendered. Try loading the `ExportUsingJavaScriptAPI.html` file and clicking on the export button while the chart is still animating. You will see that we have configured a JavaScript alert to be shown with a warning message.

Configure charts' export parameters using JavaScript

As the context menu allowed us to select whether to export the chart as an image or as PDF, we needed to do something similar when exported by clicking buttons.

Time for action – create separate buttons to export the chart as image and PDF

1. Create a copy of `ExportUsingJavaScriptAPI.html` and save it as `ExportUsingJavaScriptAPI2.html`

2. Open this file in a text editor and replace the entire `beginExportChart` function with the following modified variant:

```
function beginChartExport (format) {
  if(chartObj.hasRendered && chartObj.hasRendered()) {
    chartObj.exportChart({
      exportFormat: format
    });
    document.getElementById("exporterContainer").innerHTML = "";
  }
  else {
    alert("Please wait for the chart to render.");
  }
}
```

3. Locate the HTML button to export the chart (around line 51) and replace it with the following code, having two buttons:

```
<input type="button" value="Export Chart as Image"
  onclick="beginChartExport('PNG')" />
<input type="button" value="Export Chart as PDF"
  onclick="beginChartExport('PDF')" />
```

4. Open the file in a web browser, click on the first button labeled **Export Chart as Image**, and let the export process complete.

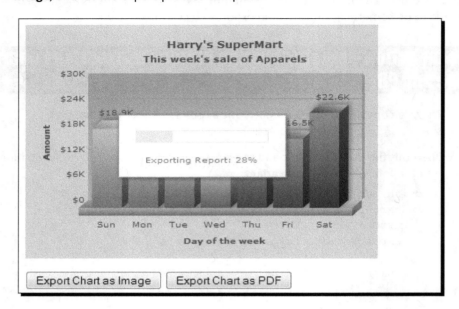

5. On completion of the export process, click on the **Save Report** button and notice that the file being saved, `SuperMart Report.png`, is an image file. You may save the file and open it using an image viewer to verify this.

6. Now click on the button labeled **Export Chart as PDF** and the same export process will begin.

7. On completion of the second export process, again click on the **Save Report** button and notice that this time the file being saved, `SuperMart Report.pdf`, is a PDF document. You may save the file and open it using a PDF document viewer to verify this.

What just happened?

To customize the export format, we tweaked our `beginChartExport` function to accept the export format as a parameter. We then went on to replace the single export button with two separate buttons that passed on the format in which the chart has to be exported.

The `exportChart` function of the chart accepts a parameter that allows us to provide export-related configurations to the chart for that particular call. Thus, even when the data of the chart explicitly states certain export-related configurations, the same can be overridden via the `exportChart` function. For example, if a chart has the attributes,

`<chart … exportAtClient="1" exportFileName="My exported chart" …>`, the same can be easily ignored and overridden by calling `chartObject.exportChart({ exportAtClient: "0", exportFileName="My new file name" });`. These configurations are temporary and are applicable only for the export call in which they were passed. If the context menu is used, the chart will again revert to the configuration passed on to it by the chart data.

For our `beginChartExport` function, we provided the export format by passing on the `exportFormat` attribute as `'PNG'` and `'PDF'` depending upon which button was clicked. There are seven other parameters, listed in the following table, which can be passed to further customize export calls:

Property Name	Purpose
`exportHandler`	This allows you to configure the ID of the export component to which the chart should forward the chart's exported image.
`exportAtClient`	One can configure whether the exported data of a chart is to be forwarded to an export component on the same page for client-side export, or to post it to a server for server-side processing.
`exportFormat`	This allows you to configure the format in which the chart has to be exported. It can accept either of the three supported export formats; JPG, PNG, or PDF.
`exportFileName`	The default filename of the exported chart can be configured using this attribute.
`exportAction`	In case of server-side exporting, the `exportAction` attribute specifies whether the exported image will be sent back to the client as a download, or whether it'll be saved on the server. The value for this attribute can be `download` or `save`.
`exportTargetWindow`	Again, in the case of server-side exporting and when using `download` as the export action, this lets you configure whether the returned image or PDF will open in the same window (as an attachment for download), or whether it will open in a new window. The value for this attribute can be `_self` or `_blank`.
`showExportDialog`	One can decide whether to show the export progress dialog when the chart is being exported. If not, the chart starts capturing the process without the dialog being visible.
`exportCallback`	When the export process is complete, the chart executes the `FC_Exported` event. The name of this callback function can be modified by using this attribute. This helps when a chart has different variants of the export methods that require different ways to handle when the export is complete.

If a chart has already been exported, then initiating a second export with the previous export component still being visible might create confusion. Hence, with the `beginChartExport` function, we deleted the contents of the export component container by executing `document.getElementById("exporterContainer").innerHTML = "";`. The export component will get rendered again as the chart will again fire the `exportReady` event upon the completion of the second export call.

Pop quiz – JavaScript Export API

1. Which chart function will you call to initiate the export process?

2. Which XML/JSON chart attribute would you use to configure the filename of the exported chart?

3. What is the name of the simple chart event that is raised when a chart completes capturing itself?

Export charts directly to the server

We wanted to provide Harry with another method to share the exported charts—distributing a URL of the saved chart image. For this, we will utilize the ability of FusionCharts to send the exported chart directly to a server.

The process of exporting charts and saving them on the server involves setting up a server-side export component on your server. The client-side export component SWF and its associated JavaScript file are redundant for server-side export. The charts, after being rendered locally within a browser window, send the exported data to the server-side component, which in turn converts this data to image or PDF files. This file can be sent back to the browser for download or be saved on the server for later use.

Depending upon the supported technology of your server, you have four flavors of export component to choose from; PHP, ASP.NET, J2EE, and Ruby on Rails (RoR). The export components are located within the `ExportHandlers` folder inside the download package.

The export component scripts are to be copied to a server and should be available via a URL. For testing the implementation of Harry's audit report, we are going to assume that we have a local PHP web server, referred as `http://localhost/` as the domain URL. You can set up your own local PHP server (Apache); if you are on Windows then `http://www.wampserver.com/` or `http://php.iis.net/` can be a good place to start, and for Mac, you may want to take a look at `http://www.mamp.info/`. Otherwise, you can use a remote web server if you have the FTP access for the same.

Time for action – configure the server-side export handler

1. Create a folder within the HTTP root of your server and name it as `Export`. This folder should be accessible as `http://<<yourdomain>>/Export/`. For our case, it would be `http://localhost/Export/`.

2. In case your folder name is not `Export`, or it is not the root of your server, then ensure that the uploaded `FCExporter.php` is edited to reflect the changes in the definition of `SAVE_PATH` and `HTTP_URI`.

3. Upload or copy the contents of the `/ExportHandlers/PHP/` folder from the download package to this newly created folder on your server.

4. Verify that the file `FCExporter.php` is accessible via your web browser. For our sample, `http://localhost/Export/FCExporter.php` should refer to the file that you have just placed on the server. This is your export handler URL.

5. Create another folder on the server within the `Export` folder and name it as `ExportedImages`. This is where the exporter will store the saved images by default.

6. Set *write* permissions for this `ExportedImages` folder. For Linux-based systems, it can be done by executing `CHMOD 777` on this folder. For Windows, appropriate security settings are to be set. In case you are not aware of how to set the write permissions, you will need to contact your web hosting provider or read your server documentation.

What just happened?

For the charts to be able to export to the server, we set up the FusionCharts server-side export component on our server root, under the folder named Export. The process was as easy as simply uploading the export handler files (available within the FusionCharts download package) to the server and making sure it was accessible via a URL.

 If your server technology is not PHP, then the process to set up an export component for your server will be slightly different. The documentation section **Exporting Charts as PDF or Images | Server-side Export | Saving Exported Output on Server Disk** explains this in detail.

As our export component will be saving the files to the server, we need to ensure that our server has write permission to the `Export/ExportedImages` folder.

Time for action – create a button to perform server-side export of the chart

1. Create a copy of `CustomizeClientSideExport.html` and save it as `ExportToServer.html`

2. Open this newly created HTML file with a text editor and append the following lines of code to the working `<script>` block (around line 44):

```
function exportChartToServer () {
  if(chartObj.hasRendered && chartObj.hasRendered()) {
    chartObj.exportChart({
      exportAtClient: '0',
      exportHandler: 'http://localhost/Export/FCExporter.php',
      exportCallback: 'showExportUrl',
      exportAction: 'save'
    });
    document.getElementById("exporterContainer").innerHTML =
      "Exporting chart to server. Please wait...";
  }
  else {
    alert("Please wait for the chart to render.");
  }
}

function showExportUrl (exportResult) {
  if (exportResult.statusCode == "1"){
    document.getElementById("exporterContainer").innerHTML =
      "Chart uploaded to <a href='http://localhost/Export/"+
        exportResult.fileName + "'>this link</a>."
  }
  else {
    alert("The chart could not be saved on server. " + "There was
      an error.\n\n" + exportResult.statusMessage);
    document.getElementById("exporterContainer").innerHTML = "";
  }
}
```

3. In case your export handler URL is not the default one we have assumed, modify the same for the `exportHandler` attribute that we passed on to the chart (around line 48.) Also, note that the domain of the URL shown when the chart exports (around line 63), needs to be modified with the path to your export handler.

4. Add a new button after the two client-side export buttons (around line 81). Type the following lines of code:

```
<input type="button" value="Export Chart to server"
  onclick="exportChartToServer()" />
```

5. Open the HTML file within a web browser and click on the button labeled **Export Chart to server**. The export process will begin and a text will appear under the chart asking you to wait until the export process completes, as shown in the following screenshot:

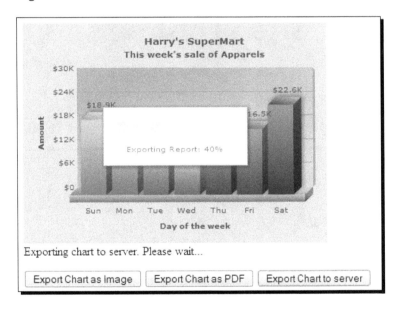

6. Once the exporting process is complete, the data will be posted to the server and after that, the URL of the uploaded chart will appear under the chart, as shown in the following screenshot (in case you see an error message, the error message will be displayed with hints to the source of the problem):

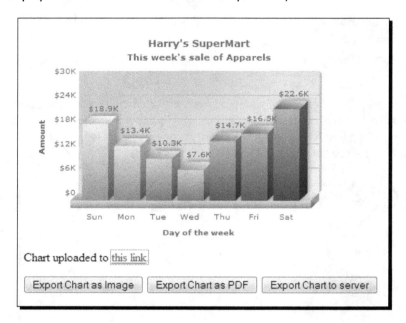

7. Click on the link and the exported image will open.

What just happened?

Once our server-side export component was set up, our next step involved creating a JavaScript function to initiate a server-side export. We created the function `exportChartToServer` to initiate the export with a different set of export configurations.

The updated export configuration had `exportAtClient` set to `0`, instructing the chart to send the exported data to a server instead of forwarding it to the export component `SWF`. We also sent the reference to the server-side export handler by providing the URL of `FCExporter.php` to the `exportHandler` attribute.

Once the data is sent to the server, we had to save it on the server's disk. This was instructed by the `exportAction: "save"` configuration. Had we not provided this, the server-side export component would simply return the file to the browser to be downloaded locally.

If the `exportAction` parameter is not defined or set to `"download"`, the export component does not save the exported chart within the server. Instead, the exported chart image is sent back to the browser for download. This can be useful if you want to save the chart without using the additional client-side export component SWF file.

Finally, once the export process was complete, we had to show a message with the location of the file saved on the server. Upon completion of the export process, the chart executes a callback function and passes the status information regarding the export process. We specified the name of this callback function using the `exportCallback` attribute and set it as `exportCallback: "showExportUrl"`.

Subsequently, we created a function called `showExportUrl`. This function accepted the export status as its only parameter. The export status is passed on as an object containing the following keys:

Property Name	Description
statusCode	This signifies whether the export process was successful or not. In case of a successful export, the status code is `1` and in case of a failure it is `0`.
statusMessage	If the export process was not successful, the status message contains a string specifying the reason for the failure.
fileName	The export component has the ability to rename a file in case a file already exists on the server with the specified export filename. Thus, on a successful export, the filename is returned back to the chart, so that the possibly changed filename can be utilized.
width	Specifies the width of the saved image.
height	Specifies the height of the saved image.
DOMId	This contains the ID of the source chart whose exported image has been saved on the server.

In our `showExportUrl` function, we first checked whether the `statusCode` was equal to `1`. If yes, then we went on to update the export component container with a message containing the URL of the exported chart. Had the export failed, we would have coded the function to show a JavaScript alert showing the status message.

The JavaScript variant of FusionCharts can be exported at server-side by simply setting `exportEnabled="1"` within chart data XML/JSON. The documentation section **Exporting as Image/PDF | Exporting Pure JavaScript Charts** explains how to customize this process.

Exporting charts without a browser

Using the community-driven plugin FCImg, FusionCharts can be exported completely at server-side without having to first render them within a browser. Head over to the plugin's website at `http://fcimg.org/` to know more.

Have a go hero – put the export features to use

We have completed developing all export related features that Harry would need in his audit report page. Why not integrate these with the final audit report page that we created in *Chapter 3, JavaScript Capabilities*?

Heads up:

- The three XML data of the final audit report (of *Chapter 3, JavaScript Capabilities*) need to be updated with additional export related chart attributes.

- Additional export component scripts are to be added to the page head.

- The script and HTML elements from this chapter are to be copied over. Ensure that you rename the variables to match the final script.

- Since the final audit report page has three charts that can dynamically update, we need to ensure that we tap into the `DataUpdated` event, and clear the export component every time the chart reloads.

Summary

In this chapter, we explored all the exporting capabilities of a chart.

Specifically, we covered the following:

- Exporting charts client-side within the browser. We implemented the FusionCharts Export Component to enable the saving of the chart as an image and a PDF

- Using the chart's JavaScript API to control the chart's export process

- Saving a chart's exported image to the server

Finally, we took on the assignment of integrating whatever we learned in this chapter with the audit report page that we are developing for Harry's SuperMart.

Having trawled through all the capabilities and JavaScript API of FusionCharts, we will now go ahead to look into how well FusionCharts can be integrated with server-side scripts.

6
Integrating with Server-side Scripts

Harry's appetite for data visualization has been growing since he saw his first chart. He loves the fact that technology can help him get more insights into his business, and he wants to stretch it further. Till now, whenever Harry needed a chart, we had to manually request data from Harry's team, convert it to FusionCharts XML or JSON format, and then build the chart for Harry. This would result in a time lag, which Harry now wants to eliminate.

Harry is curious to know if we can connect the charts directly to his databases and create them dynamically, so that whenever he views the chart, it shows the latest data. We will help him discover and execute his goal using FusionCharts. We will help him build dynamic charts that are connected to his database using a server-side script, and hence are always up-to-date without requiring any manual effort.

In this chapter, you will:

◆ Learn how to embed FusionCharts dynamically in ASP.NET, PHP, and JSP

◆ Create a chart dynamically using data stored in arrays

◆ Create a chart driven by data stored in a database

◆ Add drill-down functionality to the charts powered by data from the database

FusionCharts and server-side scripts

If you recall from *Chapter 1, Introducing FusionCharts*, building a chart involved three steps:

1. Set up FusionCharts for the entire application, typically done only once per application.

2. Encode the data for the chart, either in XML or JSON format.

3. Write the HTML and JavaScript code to include the chart in a web page.

Setting FusionCharts for your dynamic web application

Setting up FusionCharts for your server-side application is very similar to what we have discussed in *Chapter 1, Introducing FusionCharts*. The easiest way is to create a globally accessible folder called `Charts` or `FusionCharts` in the root of your web application, and then copy all the SWF and JavaScript files from the `/Charts` folder of the FusionCharts download package to this folder.

Embedding FusionCharts in a web page without using JavaScript

Before we get to the data encoding part, let's review the last step, that is, embedding the chart in a page. You can still use the following JavaScript code to embed the chart in your dynamic web page, which we have been using throughout:

```
<script type="text/javascript"><!--
  var myChart = new FusionCharts("../FusionCharts/Column3D.swf",
  "myChartId", "400", "300", "0", "1" );
  myChart.setXMLUrl("Data.xml");
  myChart.render("chartContainer");
  // -->
</script>
```

However, if you do not want to dabble in JavaScript and wish there was a way you could write this code in your own programming language, FusionCharts lets you do just that using ready-made libraries provided for ASP, C#, VB.NET, ColdFusion, J2EE, PHP, and Ruby on Rails. These libraries help you write the chart embedding code without dabbling in JavaScript. These libraries are present in the FusionCharts download package, under the folder `/Code/{Technology Name}`. Note that you will still be required to include `FusionCharts.js` in your web page, as these libraries internally generate the JavaScript code for you that uses `FusionCharts.js`. We will soon see how to use these libraries. Before that, let's first understand how to connect the charts to dynamic data.

Dynamic data and FusionCharts

Typically, in a web application, data is stored in, or requested from, the following sources:

- Databases, for example, MySQL, Microsoft SQL Server, Oracle, and so on
- Web services invoked through an API
- Other storage formats such as XML and CSV
- Internal data structures such as arrays and enumerations

However, FusionCharts accepts data in two formats only, namely XML or JSON. Additionally, the XML and JSON data is structured differently for single series and multi-series charts.

This requires you to convert the data stored in databases, web services or any of the aforementioned sources to FusionCharts XML or JSON format. This is done in server-side scripts that we will write in programming languages such as ASP.NET, PHP, JSP, and so on. These scripts connect to your database or other data sources, read the data, process it, convert it to XML or JSON, and finally provide it to the chart. As all of this happens outside the purview of FusionCharts, it enables FusionCharts to work with any server-side script or datasource, as long as the XML or JSON data provided to it is valid and structured for the chart type.

As we have earlier seen, the data can be provided to FusionCharts in two ways:

1. As a URL, using `setXMLURL()` or `setJSONUrl()` methods, termed as the **Data URL method**.
2. As a String, using the `setXMLData()` or `setJSONData()` methods, termed as the **Data String method**.

When using the Data URL method, you instruct FusionCharts to load the XML or JSON data from a URL. This URL could refer to a static XML file that is already present on the server, or it could refer to a virtual data provider, for example, `/path_to/DataProvider.php`, which when executed, queries the database, builds the XML data as string, and finally outputs this XML string to the output stream with content type set to `text/xml`, but without any HTML tags.

When using the Data String method, the XML or JSON data gets embedded in the web page, along with the chart's JavaScript code. This reduces the effort to create a static data file or a virtual data provider. Another advantage is that the chart does not have to wait for data loading once the page containing the chart has finished loading, as the data is present locally within the page. For the sake of simplicity, we will use this method in the chapter.

Now that you are familiar with the basics, let's quickly define the scope of our charts, which charts will be we creating, and in which languages.

Scope of our dynamic charts and the basic setup

In this chapter, we will use three common server-side scripting languages—PHP, ASP.NET using C#, and JSP. In each of these languages, we will create the following dynamic charts:

- As our simplest example, we will create a chart using data stored in arrays. This will help you understand how to convert data dynamically to XML. We will compare the Sales of Food Products to Non-Food Products in this chart.

- Next, we will build the same from the data stored in a sample database. In this chart, we will replicate the annual revenue that we had earlier built, but this time the data will come from a database. We will use a simple database for this, as explained in the following section.

- Finally, we will add drill-down capabilities to the previously created chart to allow Harry to drill-down from annual revenues to quarterly revenues.

Time for action – getting ready to build dynamic charts

1. Ensure that you have a ready application in PHP, ASP.NET, or JSP in which you want to use FusionCharts. For the sake of brevity, we will not cover how to create or set up a new application. You can use your choice of IDE for the application creation and coding.

2. Create a new database (recommended) or use an existing database, which we will use to create dynamic charts. Next, download `harrys_supermarket.sql` which is present in the downloads of this book and execute the SQL scripts contained in this file against your database. This script creates just one table `orders`, having four columns, namely, `order_id`, `cust_id`, `order_date`, and `order_amount`, as shown in the following table:

order_id	cust_id	order_date	order_amount
476	692	2010-06-15	1134
789	991	2011-05-24	5999
1134	1250	2011-09-30	499
....	....	....	....

The SQL script also populates the table with dummy data. We will use this table to create our dynamic charts. In a real-life database, this table would typically represent one of the many tables related to e-commerce, but the basic concepts of creating a chart would not change.

3. Set up FusionCharts for your application by copying the JS and SWF files from the `{FusionCharts download package}/Charts` folder to a newly created `Charts` or `FusionCharts` folder in the root of your web application.

Now you are all set to build charts for your dynamic web applications using FusionCharts. Let us first explore how to do it in PHP.

Creating FusionCharts in PHP

We will first create a multi-series Column 3D chart to represent the Sales of Food Products versus Non-Food Products for 2009, 2010, and 2011. To focus on the conversion of data to XML, we have stored data for this example in PHP arrays.

Time for action – creating a chart using data from array

1. In the root of your web application, create a folder named `Includes` if you do not already have it, and copy the FusionCharts PHP Library `FusionCharts.php` and `DBConn.php` files from FusionCharts download package | `Code | PHP | Includes`.

2. Create a PHP file named `chart_from_array.php` in the root of your application.

3. Type the following code in it:

```
<?php
   include("/Includes/FusionCharts.php");
?>
<html>
   <head>
      <title>FusionCharts - Plotting data from an array</title>
      <script src="Charts/FusionCharts.js"></script>
   </head>
   <body>
      <?php
         $productArray = array();
         $productArray['2009']['Sales of Food Products'] = 892500;
         $productArray['2010']['Sales of Food Products'] = 1407400;
         $productArray['2011']['Sales of Food Products'] = 1565000;
         $productArray['2009']['Sales of Non-Food Products'] =
            595000;
         $productArray['2010']['Sales of Non-Food Products'] =
            693200;
         $productArray['2011']['Sales of Non-Food Products'] =
            880400;
         $strXML = "<chart caption='Break-up of sales for last 3
```

```
              years' numberPrefix='$'>";
      $strXML .= "<categories>";
      foreach($productArray as $product => $name) {
        $strXML .= "<category label = '".$product."'/>";
      }
      $strXML .= "</categories>";
      $strXML .= "<dataset seriesName='Sales of Food Products'>";
      foreach($productArray as $product => $name) {
        $strXML .= "<set value = '".$name['Sales of Food
          Products']."'/>";
      }
      $strXML .= "</dataset>";
      $strXML .= "<dataset seriesName='Sales of Non-Food
        Products'>";
      foreach($productArray as $product => $name) {
        $strXML .= "<set value = '".$name['Sales of Non-Food
          Products']."'/>";
      }
      $strXML .= "</dataset>";
      $strXML .= "</chart>";
      echo renderChart("Charts/MSColumn3D.swf", "", $strXML,
        "productSales", 600, 300, false, true);
    ?>
  </body>
</html>
```

4. Now navigate to this page from your web browser. Go to http://path_to_your_app/chart_from_array.php. You should see the following chart:

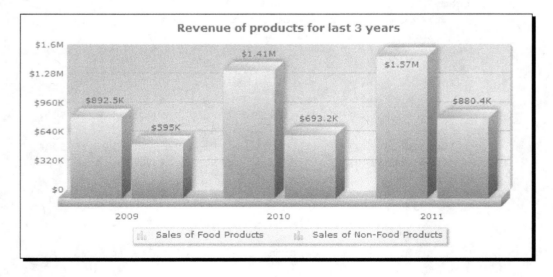

What just happened?

Bingo! We just created our first data-driven chart in PHP. Let us break down the code into bits for easier understanding.

First up, we included the FusionCharts PHP Library using the following code. This library contains helper methods that let you create a chart without having to dabble with JavaScript.

```
include("/Includes/FusionCharts.php");
```

Thereafter, we included `FusionCharts.js` in the page. This is essential for the chart to be created.

```
<script src="Charts/FusionCharts.js"></script>
```

Next, we created an associative array to store the data for this chart. While a normal array would have faster performance, for the sake of easier understanding we have used an associative array. We store data for two categories of items—Food Products and Non-food Products for three years, as shown in the following code snippet:

```
$productArray = array();
  $productArray['2009']['Sales of Food Products'] = 892500;
  $productArray['2010']['Sales of Food Products'] = 1407400;
  $productArray['2011']['Sales of Food Products'] = 1565000;
  $productArray['2009']['Sales of Non-Food Products'] = 595000;
  $productArray['2010']['Sales of Non-Food Products'] = 693200;
  $productArray['2011']['Sales of Non-Food Products'] = 880400;
```

Next is the most crucial part where we are converting this data into XML. To do so, we create a string called `$strXML` and initialize it with the `<chart>` element and the requisite attributes for this chart.

```
$strXML = "<chart caption='Break-up of sales for last 3 years'
  numberPrefix='$'>";
```

To add the x-axis labels, we need to create the `<categories>` and `<category>` elements, which is done using the following code. In this code, we iterate through our array and add `2009`, `2010`, and `2011` as the x-axis labels.

```
$strXML .= "<categories>";
foreach($productArray as $product => $name) {
  $strXML .= "<category label = '".$product."'/>";
}
$strXML .= "</categories>";
```

Thereafter, we add the XML element `<dataset>` for two data series, namely Food Products and Non-Food Products, and also the data points under each data series as the `<set>` element. To do this, we iterate through our array again.

```
$strXML .= "<dataset seriesName='Sales of Food Products'>";
foreach($productArray as $product => $name) {
    $strXML .= "<set value = '".$name['Sales of Food Products']."'/>";
}
$strXML .= "</dataset>";
$strXML .= "<dataset seriesName='Sales of Non-Food Products'>";
foreach($productArray as $product => $name) {
    $strXML .= "<set value = '".$name['Sales of Non-Food
        Products']."'/>";
}
$strXML .= "</dataset>";
```

Finally, we append the closing `</chart>` element to the string variable. If, at this point in time, you have seen the contents of `$strXML`, you will have seen the entire XML for our multi-series chart.

The only thing left is to embed the chart in the page, for which we use the `renderChart()` method provided by FusionCharts PHP Library, instead of direct JavaScript code, as in the following code:

```
echo renderChart("Charts/MSColumn3D.swf", "", $strXML,
    "productSales", 600, 300, false, true);
```

Here, we are creating a multi-series Column 3D chart, whose SWF is `MSColumn3D.swf`, giving it an ID of `productSales`, a width of 600 and a height of 300. We are also relaying the XML data we earlier created in `$strXML` to this chart using the Data String method. This method internally generates the complete JavaScript and HTML code to add the chart to the page as a string and returns it, hence we need to `echo` the output of this method.

When the code is now run, the XML is generated and stored in `$strXML`, and when `renderChart()` is invoked with all the parameters, it returns the code to generate a chart in our page. The `renderChart()` method takes parameters in the following order:

- Chart SWF.
- URL to static XML file, if the Data URL method is to be used. If you intend to use the Data String method, leave this as blank.
- Variable containing XML data string, if the Data String method is to be used. If you have specified data as a URL, leave this parameter blank.
- Unique ID for this chart. Each chart in a page needs to be have a unique ID.
- Width of this chart, in pixels.

- Height of this chart, in pixels.

- Boolean flag to enable Debug Mode, which lets you debug your chart if something is not working.

- Boolean flag to register the chart with the FusionCharts JavaScript object. This should be set as true.

What if you wished to render the chart as JavaScript, or provide data in JSON?

When rendering FusionCharts in PHP using the PHP library, you can choose to render the chart in JavaScript only, by adding the following code before the `renderChart()` method of the specific chart:

`FC_SetRenderer("javascript");`

Similarly, to provide JSON data to the chart, instead of XML, you can invoke the following method before the `renderChart()` method of the specific chart:

`FC_SetDataFormat("json");`

Now that we know the basics of how to create a dynamic chart, let's explore how to change the data source from an array to a database. We will use the table `orders` that we earlier created, and explained during the setup. Using the data from this table, we will create a chart that lets Harry compare the annual revenues for last three years.

Time for action – creating a chart in PHP using data from MySQL

1. Create a blank PHP file named `chart_from_mysql.php` in the root of your web application.

2. Type the following code in it:

```php
<?php
  include("/Includes/FusionCharts.php");
  include("/Includes/DBConn.php");
?>
<html>
  <head>
    <title>FusionCharts XT - Plotting data from MySQL</title>
    <script src="Charts/FusionCharts.js"></script>
  </head>
  <body>
    <center>
      <?php
        // Connect to the Database
        $link = connectToDB();
```

```
            // Fetch all total revenue of the last 3 years using SQL
               Query
            $strQuery = "SELECT SUM( order_amount ) AS SUM,
               YEAR( order_date ) AS YEAR FROM orders GROUP BY YEAR
               ( order_date )";
            $result = mysql_query($strQuery) or die(mysql_error());
            $strXML = "<chart caption='Annual Revenue - last 3 years'
               numberPrefix='$'>";
            while($row = mysql_fetch_array($result, MYSQL_BOTH)) {
               $strXML .= "<set label = '".$row['YEAR']."' value =
                  '".$row['SUM']."' />";
            }
            $strXML .= "</chart>";
            echo renderChart("Charts/Column3D.swf", "", $strXML,
               "annual_revenue", 600, 300, false, true);
         ?>
      </center>
   </body>
</html>
```

3. Run this page by going to `http://path_to_your_app/chart_from_mysql.php`. You should see the chart as in the following screenshot:

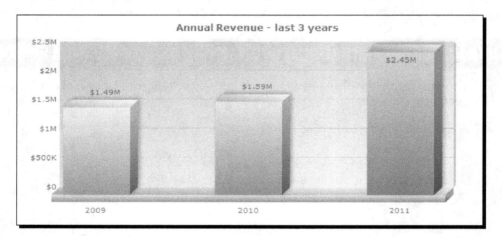

What just happened

You just created a chart by pulling in data from a MySQL database. Here is a rundown of the code.

As seen earlier, you first included FusionCharts PHP Library. This time, there is another included called `DBConn.php` that helps establish a connection to a database. It contains a `connectToDB()` function that returns a valid connection link to the MySQL database specified. In `DBConn.php`, you need to ensure that the authentication details for your database is correctly mentioned, as shown in the following lines of code:

```
$hostdb = 'localhost';     // MySQL host
$userdb = 'root';          // MySQL username
$passdb = '';              // MySQL password
$namedb = 'harrys_supermarket'; // Name of the database
```

Next, we include `FusionCharts.js` in the page, which is necessary for the chart to render.

To build the data, we now connect to the database and run the SQL query to get aggregate sales by year, using the following lines of code:

```
// Connect to the Database
  $link = connectToDB();
  // Fetch all total revenue of the last 3 years using SQL Query
  $strQuery = "SELECT SUM( order_amount ) AS SUM, YEAR( order_date )
    AS YEAR FROM orders GROUP BY YEAR( order_date )";
  $result = mysql_query($strQuery) or die(mysql_error());
```

Next, we need to convert this data into the FusionCharts XML format. For this, we again use a string `$strXML` and iterate through the recordset to add the `<set>` elements for the chart.

```
$strXML = "<chart caption='Annual Revenue - last 3 years'
  numberPrefix='$'>";
while($row = mysql_fetch_array($result, MYSQL_BOTH)) {
  $strXML .= "<set label = '".$row['YEAR']."'
    value = '".$row['SUM']."' />";
}
$strXML .= "</chart>";
```

With the XML now ready in `$strXML`, we invoke the `renderChart()` method and pass the relevant parameters to build our chart, using the following lines of code:

```
echo renderChart("Charts/Column3D.swf", "", $strXML,
  "annual_revenue", 600, 300, false, true);
```

Simple, isn't it?

Now that Harry can see his annual revenues on the chart, he will definitely want to dive deep into one of those columns and see how sales performed for each quarter of that year. To enable that, we need to add drill-down capabilities on this chart, which we will see in the following section.

Time for action – adding drill-down to a database-driven chart

1. In `chart_from_mysql.php`, modify this line of code:

```
$strXML .= "<set label = '".$row['YEAR']."'
   value = '".$row['SUM']."' link=
   'quarterly_chart_from_mysql.php?year=".$row['YEAR']."'/>";
```

2. And this line as well:

```
$strXML = "<chart caption='Annual Revenue - last 3 years'
   subCaption='Click on a column to see quarterly revenues for that
   year' numberPrefix='$'>";
```

3. Create a blank PHP file named `quarterly_chart_from_mysql.php` in the same
location. Type in the following code:

```
<?php
   include("/Includes/FusionCharts.php");
   include("/Includes/DBConn.php");
?>
<html>
   <head>
      <title>FusionCharts XT - Rendering drill-down charts from
         MySQL database</title>
      <script src="Charts/FusionCharts.js"></script>
   </head>
   <body>
      <center>
         <?php
            //Request the factory Id from QueryString
            $year = $_REQUEST['year'];
            // Connect to DB
            $link = connectToDB();
            // Fetch all revenue for each quarter for the year
               specified
            $strQuery = "SELECT SUM(order_amount) AS SUM,
               QUARTER(order_date) AS Quarter FROM orders WHERE
               YEAR(order_date) = " . $year . " AND
               QUARTER(order_date) IN (SELECT QUARTER(order_date)
               FROM orders) GROUP BY Quarter";
            $result = mysql_query($strQuery) or die(mysql_error());
            $strXML = "<chart caption='Quarterly Revenue - $year'
               numberPrefix='$'>";
            while($row = mysql_fetch_array($result, MYSQL_BOTH)) {
               $strXML .= "<set label = 'Qtr - ".$row['Quarter']."'
                  value = '".$row['SUM']."'/>";
```

```
        }
        $strXML .= "</chart>";
        echo renderChart("Charts/Column3D.swf", "", $strXML,
            "quarterly_revenue", 600, 300, false, true);
    ?>
    </center>
  </body>
</html>
```

4. To see the drill-down in action, first navigate to `http://path_to_your_ app/ chart_from_mysql.php`. Here you will see the chart showing annual revenues. Click on any of the columns. You will now see another chart showing the quarterly revenue for that year. For example, if you click on 2009, the chart will be similar to the following screenshot:

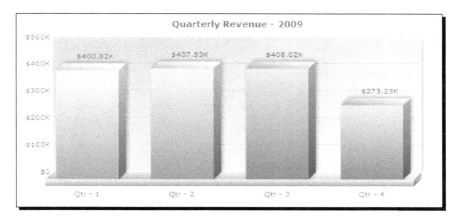

What just happened?

We enabled drill-down on the annual revenues chart whose column, when clicked, takes us to another page showing the quarterly revenues for that particular year.

To add drill-down to the first chart contained in `chart_from_mysql.php`, we added the `link` attribute to the `<set>` elements, using the following line of code:

```
$strXML .= "<set label = '".$row['YEAR']."' value = '".$row['SUM']."'
    link='quarterly_chart_from_mysql.php?year=".$row['YEAR']."'/>";
```

The link points to the PHP file `quarterly_chart_from_mysql.php` that we just created. We also pass the value of each year as a **QueryString** to this page. The `<set>` element for 2009 should look as follows, once generated:

```
<set label='2009' value=' 1487500 link='
    quarterly_chart_from_mysql.php?year=2009' />
```

As a good practice, we also inform the users that the chart supports drill-down by adding this information to the chart's subcaption, using the following line of code:

```
$strXML = "<chart caption='Annual Revenue - last 3 years'
   subCaption='Click on a column to see quarterly revenues for that
   year' numberPrefix='$'>";
```

Now, we need to create the quarterly chart in `quarterly_chart_from_mysql.php`. To do this, as earlier, we first include `FusionCharts.php`, `DBConn.php`, and `FusionCharts.js`. Next, we request the year for which we've to plot the quarterly chart. This year was passed to the page as a QueryString with the key `year` from the page `chart_from_mysql.php`. Whenever a user clicked on a column, the link that was invoked contained the year as a QueryString, using the following line code:

```
$year = $_REQUEST['year'];
```

We then connect to the database, get the quarterly revenues for the year, as present in the database, using the following code:

```
// Connect to DB
$link = connectToDB();
// Fetch all revenue for each quarter for the year specified
$strQuery = "SELECT SUM(order_amount) AS SUM, QUARTER(order_date) AS
   Quarter FROM orders WHERE YEAR(order_date) = " . $year . " AND
   QUARTER(order_date) IN (SELECT QUARTER(order_date) FROM orders)
   GROUP BY Quarter";
$result = mysql_query($strQuery) or die(mysql_error());
```

Next, we convert the recordset to XML by iterating through it, as earlier, using the following code:

```
$strXML = "<chart caption='Quarterly Revenue - $year'
   numberPrefix='$'>";
while($row = mysql_fetch_array($result, MYSQL_BOTH)) {
   $strXML .= "<set label = 'Qtr - ".$row['Quarter']."' value =
      '".$row['SUM']."'/>";
}
$strXML .= "</chart>";
```

Finally, we invoke the `renderChart()` method to render this chart.

```
echo renderChart("Charts/Column3D.swf", "", $strXML,
   "quarterly_revenue", 600, 300, false, true);
```

With this, you created a database-driven drill-down chart using PHP! You can now build multi-level dashboards in PHP using FusionCharts, with a variety of chart combinations in each page. We'll next explore how to achieve the same in ASP.NET using C#.

Have a go hero – build a dashboard for Harry

Extend our previous example to add another level of drill-down for Harry, so that he can click on any quarter to explore the monthly sales data.

instead of opening each child chart in a new page, use the LinkedCharts feature of FusionCharts , as explained in *Chapter 4, Enabling Drill-down on Charts* to allow opening in lightboxes.

Creating FusionCharts in ASP.NET using C#

What if Harry has the server running on ASP.NET rather than PHP? What if he has Microsoft SQL Server as his database rather than MySQL?

Just as we used the `FusionCharts.php` library to render charts in PHP, in ASP.NET we will make use of `FusionCharts.dll`, provided in the FusionCharts download package | Code | C# | bin. This DLL provides a `FusionCharts.RenderChart()` function that helps you render a chart in ASP.NET, without having to dabble in JavaScript.

As seen earlier, let us first create a chart in ASP.NET using C#. To do this, we will first create a new project and configure it to use `FusionCharts.dll`.

Time for action – using FusionCharts.dll in a new Visual Studio project

1. Fire up Visual Studio, and create a blank ASP.NET (C#) website. Save the project as `Harrys_Supermarket`.

2. Right-click the project's name in **Solution Explorer** | **Add New Item** | **Web Form**. Rename it to `ArrayExample.aspx` for our first example that we will soon build.

3. Copy the `Charts` folder from the FusionCharts download package, and paste it in Solution Explorer.

4. Right-click the project's name in **Solution Explorer** and select **Add Reference**. In the window that pops up, click on the **Browse** tab, and navigate to the FusionCharts download package | Code | CS | bin | FusionCharts.dll. This will create a `bin` folder in **Solution Explorer**, and will have the `FusionCharts.dll` file in it.

What just happened

We just prepared this project to use `FusionCharts.dll`, and now we are ready to create our first chart. For our first chart, we will create a multi-series Column 3D chart to represent the Sales of Food Products versus Non-Food Products for 2009, 2010, and 2011. To focus on the conversion of data to XML, we have stored the data for this example in an array.

Time for action – create a chart in C# using data from an array

1. Open the previously created `ArrayExample.aspx`.

2. Include `FusionCharts.js` in this page by adding the code:

```
<script type="text/javascript"
  src="Charts/FusionCharts.js"></script>
```

3. Add a literal control to the form in this file, so that the code looks as:

```
<form id="form1" runat="server">
  <asp:Literal ID="Literal1" runat="server"></asp:Literal>
</form>
```

4. Open the code-behind file `ArrayExample.aspx.cs` and type in the following code:

```
using System;
using System.Collections.Generic;
using System.Linq;
using System.Web;
using System.Web.UI;
using System.Web.UI.WebControls;
using System.Text;
using InfoSoftGlobal;
public partial class _ArrayExample : System.Web.UI.Page
{
  protected void Page_Load(object sender, EventArgs e)
  {
    string[,] arrData = {
      { "Sales of Food Products", "892500", "2009" },
      { "Sales of Non-Food Products", "595000", "2009" },
      { "Sales of Food Products", "1407400", "2010" },
      { "Sales of Non-Food Products", "693200", "2010" },
      { "Sales of Food Products", "1565000", "2011" },
      { "Sales of Non-Food Products", "880400", "2011" },
    };
    StringBuilder xmlStr = new StringBuilder();
    xmlStr.Append("<chart caption='Break-up of sales for last 3
```

```
      years' numberPrefix='$'>");
    xmlStr.Append("<categories>");
    for (int i = 0; i < 6; i++)
    {
      xmlStr.AppendFormat("<category label = '{0}' />", arrData[i,
        2]);
      i++;
    }
    xmlStr.Append("</categories>");
    xmlStr.Append("<dataset seriesName = 'Sales of Food
      Products'>");
    for (int i = 0; i < 3; i++)
    {
      xmlStr.AppendFormat("<set value = '{0}' />", arrData[i, 1]);
    }
    xmlStr.Append("</dataset>");
    xmlStr.Append("<dataset seriesName = 'Sales of Non-Food
      Products'>");
    for (int i = 3; i < 6; i++)
    {
      xmlStr.AppendFormat("<set value = '{0}' />", arrData[i, 1]);
    }
    xmlStr.Append("</dataset>");
    xmlStr.Append("</chart>");
    Literal1.Text = FusionCharts.RenderChart
      ("FusionCharts/MSColumn3D.swf", "", xmlStr.ToString(),
      "productSales", "600", "300", false, true);
  }
}
```

5. View this page in a browser, and you'll see the same chart as before.

What just happened

You just created a data-driven chart in C#. Let us explore how we did it.

In `ArrayExample.aspx`, we included `FusionCharts.js` by adding the following line of code:

```
<script src="Charts/FusionCharts.js"></script>
```

Thereafter, we added a `Literal` control to the page, which acted as a container for the chart. The code-behind page `ArrayExample.aspx.cs` will place the chart in this `Literal`.

```
<form id="form1" runat="server">
      <asp:Literal ID="Literal1" runat="server"></asp:Literal>
</form>
```

In the code-behind page, we first include the FusionCharts C# assembly `FusionCharts.dll` contained in the `InfoSoftGlobal` namespace using the following code. This assembly contains helper methods that let you create a chart without having to dabble in JavaScript.

```
using InfoSoftGlobal;
```

Next, we created an associative array to store the data for this chart. While a normal array would have faster performance, for the sake of easier understanding we have used an associative array. We store data for two categories of items—Food Products and Non-Food Products, for three years, using the following code:

```
string[,] arrData = {
    { "Sales of Food Products", "892500", "2009" },
    { "Sales of Non-Food Products", "595000", "2009" },
    { "Sales of Food Products", "1407400", "2010" },
    { "Sales of Non-Food Products", "693200", "2010" },
    { "Sales of Food Products", "1565000", "2011" },
    { "Sales of Non-Food Products", "880400", "2011" },
};
```

Next is the most crucial part where we are converting this data into XML. To do so, we create a string called `xmlStr` and initialize it with the `<chart>` element and requisite attributes for this chart. We use the `StringBuilder` class for our string operations.

```
StringBuilder xmlStr = new StringBuilder();
xmlStr.Append("<chart caption='Break-up of sales for last 3 years'
    numberPrefix='$'>");
```

To add the x-axis labels, we need to create the `<categories>` and `<category>` elements, which is done using the following code. In this code, we iterate through our array and add `2009`, `2010`, and `2011` as the x-axis labels, as in the following code:

```
xmlStr.Append("<categories>");
for (int i = 0; i < 6; i++)
{
    xmlStr.AppendFormat("<category label = '{0}' />", arrData[i, 2]);
    i++;
}
xmlStr.Append("</categories>");
```

Thereafter, we add the XML element `<dataset>` for two data series, namely Food Products and Non-Food Products, and also the data points under each data series as `<set>` element. To do this, we iterate through our array again, using the following code:

```
xmlStr.Append("<dataset seriesName = 'Sales of Food Products'>");
for (int i = 0; i < 3; i++)
{
```

```
    xmlStr.AppendFormat("<set value = '{0}' />", arrData[i, 1]);
  }
xmlStr.Append("</dataset>");
xmlStr.Append("<dataset seriesName = 'Sales of Non-Food Products'>");
for (int i = 3; i < 6; i++)
{
    xmlStr.AppendFormat("<set value = '{0}' />", arrData[i, 1]);
}
xmlStr.Append("</dataset>");
```

Finally, we append the closing `</chart>` element to the string variable. If, at this point in time, you have seen the contents of `xmlStr`, you will have seen the entire XML for our multi-series chart.

The only thing left is to embed the chart in the page, for which we use the `RenderChart()` method provided by `FusionCharts.dll`, instead of direct JavaScript code. We assign the string value returned by this method to `Literal`, that acts as chart placeholder.

```
Literal1.Text = FusionCharts.RenderChart("Charts/MSColumn3D.swf", "",
    xmlStr.ToString(), "productSales", "600", "300", false, true);
```

Here, we are creating a multi-series Column 3D chart, whose SWF is `MSColumn3D.swf`, giving it an ID of `productSales`, a width of 600 and height of 300. We are also relaying the XML data we earlier created in `$strXML` to this chart using the Data String method. This method internally generates the complete JavaScript and HTML code to add the chart to the page as a string and returns it; hence we assign it to `Literal1.Text`.

When the code is now run, the XML is generated and stored in `xmlStr`, and when `RenderChart()` is invoked with all the parameters, it returns the code to generate a chart in our page. The `RenderChart()` method in `FusionCharts.dll` takes in parameters, similar to the one in `FusionCharts.php`, as explained earlier.

What if you wished to render the chart as JavaScript, or provide data in JSON?

When rendering FusionCharts in ASP.NET using `FusionCharts.dll`, you can choose to render the chart in JavaScript only, by adding the following code before the `RenderChart()` method of the specific chart:

```
FusionCharts.SetRenderer("javascript");
```

Similarly, to provide JSON data to the chart, instead of XML, you can invoke the following method before the `RenderChart()` method of the specific chart:

```
FusionCharts.SetDataFormat("json");
```

Now that we know the basics of how to create a dynamic chart, let's explore how to change the datasource from an array to a database. We will use the table `orders` that we earlier created, but this time using SQL Server. Using the data from this table, we will create a chart that lets Harry compare the annual revenues for the last three years.

Time for action – creating a chart in ASP.NET using data from an SQL Server

1. Create a new file in your project and name it as `AnnualRevenues.aspx`.

2. Include `FusionCharts.js` in this page by adding the code:

```
<script type="text/javascript"
  src="Charts/FusionCharts.js"></script>
```

3. Add a literal control to the form in this file, so that the code is similar to the following:

```
<form id="form1" runat="server">
  <asp:Literal ID="l1" runat="server"></asp:Literal>
</form>
```

4. Open the code-behind file `AnnualRevenues.aspx.cs` and type in the following code:

```
using System;
using System.Collections.Generic;
using System.Linq;
using System.Web;
using System.Web.UI;
using System.Web.UI.WebControls;
using System.Data;
using System.Data.Sql;
using System.Data.SqlClient;
using System.Text;
using InfoSoftGlobal;
public partial class _AnnualRevenues : System.Web.UI.Page
{
  protected void Page_Load(object sender, EventArgs e)
  {
    string connStr = @"Data
      Source=.\SQLEXPRESS;AttachDbFilename=C:\Users\Fusion
      Charts\Documents\Visual Studio 2010\WebSites\Harrys
      Supermarket\App_Data\Harrys_Supermarket.mdf;Integrated
      Security=True;User Instance=True";
    StringBuilder strXML = new StringBuilder();
    strXML.Append("<chart caption='Annual Revenue - last 3 years'
```

```
        numberPrefix='$'>");
    using (SqlConnection conn = new SqlConnection(connStr)){
      conn.Open();
      SqlCommand query = new SqlCommand("SELECT SUM(order_amount)
        AS SUM, YEAR(order_date) AS YEAR FROM orders GROUP BY
        YEAR(order_date) ORDER BY YEAR(order_date)", conn);
      SqlDataReader ret_value = query.ExecuteReader();
      while (ret_value.Read())
      {
        strXML.AppendFormat("<set label='{0}' value='{1}' />",
          ret_value["YEAR"].ToString(),
          ret_value["SUM"].ToString());
      }
      strXML.Append("</chart>");
      ret_value.Close();
      conn.Close();
      l1.Text = FusionCharts.RenderChart("Charts/Column3D.swf",
        "", strXML.ToString(), "annual_revenue", "640", "340",
        false, true);
    }
  }
}
```

5. View this page in a browser. You should see the following chart:

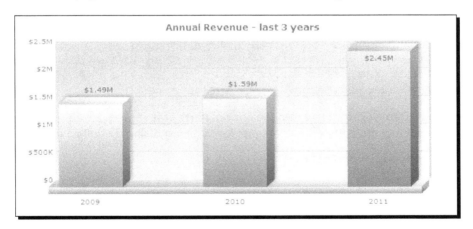

What just happened

You just created a dynamic chart in ASP.NET by pulling in data from an SQL Server database. Let's understand the code further.

In `AnnualRevenues.aspx`, we first included `FusionCharts.js`, which is necessary to render the chart. We also added a literal with the ID `11` that will act as the placeholder for the chart.

In the code-behind page, we first include `FusionCharts.dll` by including its namespace.

```
using InfoSoftGlobal;
```

To establish a connection to the database, we use the following code:

```
string connStr = @"Data
  Source=.\SQLEXPRESS;AttachDbFilename=C:\Users\Fusion
  Charts\Documents\Visual Studio 2010\WebSites\Harrys
  Supermarket\App_Data\Harrys_Supermarket.mdf;Integrated
  Security=True;User Instance=True";
```

Here, you should replace the database credentials with your own.

We also initialize a string variable `xmlStr` that will contain XML for the chart and initialize the `<chart>` element.

```
StringBuilder strXML = new StringBuilder();
strXML.Append("<chart caption='Annual Revenue - last 3 years'
  numberPrefix='$'>");
```

We now connect to the database and run the SQL query to get aggregate sales by year.

```
using (SqlConnection conn = new SqlConnection(connStr)){
  conn.Open();
  SqlCommand query = new SqlCommand("SELECT SUM(order_amount) AS SUM,
    YEAR(order_date) AS YEAR FROM orders GROUP BY YEAR(order_date)
    ORDER BY YEAR(order_date)", conn);
  SqlDataReader ret_value = query.ExecuteReader();
```

Next, we need to convert this data into the FusionCharts XML format. For this, we iterate through the recordset to add `<set>` elements for the chart, using the following code:

```
while (ret_value.Read())
{
  strXML.AppendFormat("<set label='{0}' value='{1}' />",
    ret_value["YEAR"].ToString(), ret_value["SUM"].ToString());
}
strXML.Append("</chart>");
ret_value.Close();
conn.Close();
```

With the XML now ready in `xmlStr`, we invoke the `RenderChart()` method and pass the relevant parameters to build our chart, using the following code:

```
l1.Text = FusionCharts.RenderChart("Charts/Column3D.swf", "",
  strXML.ToString(), "annual_revenue", "640", "340", false, true);
```

Simple, isn't it?

Like we did in PHP, let's now add drill-down capabilities to this chart, so that, when Harry clicks on a year's column, he can see the quarterly sales for that year.

Time for action – creating a drill-down chart in ASP.NET using data from an SQL Server

1. In `AnnualRevenues.aspx.cs`, modify this line of code:

```
strXML.AppendFormat("<set label='{0}' value='{1}' link='{2}' />",
  ret_value["YEAR"].ToString(), ret_value["SUM"].ToString(),
  "Quarterly.aspx?year=" + ret_value["YEAR"].ToString());
```

2. And this line as well:

```
strXML.Append("<chart caption='Annual Revenue - last 3 years'
  subcaption='Click on a column to view revenue for each quarter
  for that year' numberPrefix='$'>");
```

3. Add another file to this project and name it as `Quarterly.aspx`.

4. In this file, include `FusionCharts.js` by adding:

```
<script type="text/javascript"
  src="Charts/FusionCharts.js"></script>
```

5. Create a Literal control in the form tag, named as `literal1`.

```
<form id="form1" runat="server">
  <asp:Literal ID="l1" runat="server"></asp:Literal>
</form>
```

6. Open the code-behind file `Quarterly.aspx.cs` and type the following code in it:

```
using System;
using System.Collections.Generic;
using System.Linq;
using System.Web;
using System.Web.UI;
using System.Web.UI.WebControls;
using System.Data;
```

```csharp
using System.Data.Sql;
using System.Data.SqlClient;
using System.Text;
using InfoSoftGlobal;
public partial class Quarterly : System.Web.UI.Page
{
  protected void Page_Load(object sender, EventArgs e)
  {
    string year;
    year = Request["year"];
    StringBuilder strXML = new StringBuilder();
    strXML.Append("<chart caption='Quarterly Revenue - "+year+"'
      numberPrefix='$'>");
    string connStr = @"Data
      Source=.\SQLEXPRESS;AttachDbFilename=C:\Users\Fusion
      Charts\Documents\Visual Studio 2010\WebSites\Harrys
      Supermarket\App_Data\Harrys_Supermarket.mdf;Integrated
      Security=True;User Instance=True";
    using (SqlConnection conn = new SqlConnection(connStr))
    {
      conn.Open();
      SqlCommand query = new SqlCommand("SELECT SUM(order_id) AS
        SUM, DATEPART(quarter, order_date) AS Quarter FROM orders
        WHERE YEAR( order_date ) = " + year.ToString() + " AND
        DATEPART(quarter, order_date) IN (SELECT DATEPART(quarter,
        order_date) FROM orders GROUP BY DATEPART(quarter,
        order_date)) GROUP BY DATEPART(quarter, order_date) ORDER
        BY DATEPART(quarter, order_date)", conn);
      SqlDataReader r = query.ExecuteReader();
      while (r.Read())
      {
        strXML.AppendFormat("<set label='Qtr - {0}'
          value='{1}'/>", r["Quarter"].ToString(),
          r["SUM"].ToString());
      }
      strXML.Append("</chart>");
      r.Close();
      conn.Close();
      l1.Text = FusionCharts.RenderChart("Charts/Column3D.swf",
        "", strXML.ToString(), "quarterly_revenue", "640", "340",
        false, true);
    }
  }
}
```

7. Now run `AnnualRevenues.aspx`, and click on any of the columns. You should see the child chart showing the quarterly revenues for that year.

What just happened?

We enabled drill-down on the annual revenues chart, whose column when clicked takes us to another page showing quarterly revenues for the particular year.

To add drill-down to the first chart contained in `AnnualRevenues.aspx`, we added the `link` attribute to the `<set>` elements.

```
strXML.AppendFormat("<set label='{0}' value='{1}' link='{2}' />",
  ret_value["YEAR"].ToString(), ret_value["SUM"].ToString(),
  "Quarterly.aspx?year=" + ret_value["YEAR"].ToString());
```

The link points to the file `Quarterly.aspx` that we just created. We also pass the value of each year as a QueryString to this page. The `<set>` element for 2009 would look similar to the following line of code, once generated:

```
<set label='2009' value=' 1487500 link='Quarterly.aspx?year=2009' />
```

As a good practice, we also inform the users that the chart supports drill-down by adding information to chart's subcaption, using the following line of code:

```
strXML.Append("<chart caption='Annual Revenue - last 3 years'
  subcaption='Click on a column to view revenue for each quarter for
  that year' numberPrefix='$'>");
```

Now, we need to create the quarterly chart in `Quarterly.aspx`. To do this, we request the year for which we've to plot the quarterly chart. This year was passed to the page as a QueryString with the key `year` from the page `AnnualRevenues.aspx`. Whenever a user clicks on a column, the link that was invoked contains the year as a QueryString.

```
string year;
year = Request["year"];
```

We then connect to the database, and get the quarterly revenues for the year as present in the database, using the following code:

```
using (SqlConnection conn = new SqlConnection(connStr))
{
  conn.Open();
  SqlCommand query = new SqlCommand("SELECT SUM(order_id) AS SUM,
    DATEPART(quarter, order_date) AS Quarter FROM orders WHERE YEAR
    ( order_date ) = " + year.ToString() + " AND DATEPART(quarter,
    order_date) IN (SELECT DATEPART(quarter, order_date) FROM orders
    GROUP BY DATEPART(quarter, order_date)) GROUP BY
    DATEPART(quarter, order_date) ORDER BY DATEPART(quarter,
    order_date)", conn);
  SqlDataReader r = query.ExecuteReader();
```

Next, we convert the recordset to XML by iterating through it, as earlier.

```
while (r.Read())
{
  strXML.AppendFormat("<set label='Qtr - {0}' value='{1}'/>",
    r["Quarter"].ToString(), r["SUM"].ToString());
}
strXML.Append("</chart>");
```

Finally, we invoke the `RenderChart()` method to render this chart in the literal `ll`.

```
ll.Text = FusionCharts.RenderChart("Charts/Column3D.swf", "",
  strXML.ToString(), "quarterly_revenue", "640", "340", false, true);
```

With this, you created a database-driven drill-down chart using ASP.NET! You can now build multi-level dashboards in ASP.NET using FusionCharts, with a variety of chart combinations in each page. We'll next explore how to achieve the same in Java.

Have a go hero – build a dashboard for Harry

Extend our previous example to add another level of drill-down for Harry, so that he can click on any quarter to explore monthly sales data.

Instead of opening each child chart in a new page, use the LinkedCharts feature of FusionCharts to allow opening in lightboxes.

Creating charts in Java using Eclipse

Let us now build the same examples for Harry, assuming he is now using Java instead of PHP or ASP.NET.

Just as we used the `FusionCharts.php` library to render charts in PHP or `FusionCharts.dll` in ASP.NET, in the case of Java, we will make use of a set of JSTL JAR files, namely `fchelper.jar`, `fctl.jar`, `fcexporter.jar`, and `fcexporthandler.jar`, provided in the FusionCharts download package | Code | J2EE | WEB-INF | lib folder. The tag library `fctl.jar` provides helper methods that help you render a chart in your Java web applications, without having to dabble in JavaScript.

As seen earlier, let us first create a chart in Java. To do this, we will first create a new project and configure it to use the FusionCharts tag library.

Time for action – creating a new project in Eclipse and adding the tag library

1. Create a new project in Eclipse, and save it as `FusionCharts_Java_Learning`.

2. Right-click on the project and select **Properties**. Under **Java Build path**, select the **Source** tab. Click on the folder and select **Edit**. Change **src** to **WEB-INF/src** and click **Finish**.

3. Change the default output folder to `projectname/WEB-INF/classes`. Click on **OK**.

4. Create a new folder under the **WEB-INF** folder named `lib`. Copy all the `.jar` files from the download package | `Code` | `J2EE` | `WEB-INF` | `lib` here.

5. From the FusionCharts download package, copy the entire `Charts` folder to this project.

What just happened?

We just prepared this project to use the FusionCharts tag library, and now we are ready to create our first chart. For our first chart, we will create a multi-series Column 3D chart to represent the Sales of Food Products versus Non-Food Products for 2009, 2010, and 2011. To focus on the conversion of data to XML, we have stored the data for this example in an array.

Time for action – creating a chart in Java using data from an array

1. Create a new JSP file `ArrayExample.jsp` in the project.

2. Type the following code in it:

```
<!DOCTYPE HTML PUBLIC "-//W3C//DTD HTML 4.01 Transitional//EN"
  "http://www.w3.org/TR/html4/loose.dtd">
<%@ taglib prefix="c" uri="http://java.sun.com/jsp/jstl/core"%>
<%@ taglib prefix="tags" tagdir="/WEB-INF/tags"%>
<%@ taglib uri="http://www.fusioncharts.com/jsp/core"
  prefix="fc"%>
<html>
  <head>
    <title>Creating a chart in Java from an array</title>
    <script type="text/javascript"
      src="Charts/FusionCharts.js"></script>
  </head>
  <body>
  <%
```

```
        String[][] arrData = new String [3][3];
        arrData[0][0] = "2009";
        arrData[1][0] = "2010";
        arrData[2][0] = "2011";
        arrData[0][1] = "892500";
        arrData[1][1] = "815300";
        arrData[2][1] = "1407400";
        arrData[0][2] = "595000";
        arrData[1][2] = "693200";
        arrData[2][2] = "880400";
        String xmlData = "<chart caption='Break-up of sales for last 3
          years' numberPrefix='$'>";
        xmlData +=  " <categories> ";
        for (int i = 0; i <= 2; i++) {
          xmlData += " <category label ='" + arrData[i][0] + "'/> ";
        }
        xmlData += "</categories>";
        xmlData += "<dataset seriesName='Sales of Food Products'>";
        for(int i = 0; i <= 2; i++) {
          xmlData += "<set value = '" + arrData[i][1] + "'/>";
        }
        xmlData += "</dataset>";
        xmlData += "<dataset seriesName='Sales of Non-Food
          Products'>";
        for(int i = 0; i <= 2; i++) {
          xmlData += "<set value = '" + arrData[i][1] + "'/>";
        }
        xmlData += "</dataset>";
        xmlData += "</chart>";
    %>
    <c:set var="strXML" value="<%=xmlData%>" />
    test:${strXML}
    <fc:render chartId="chart_from_array"
      swfFilename="Charts/MSColumn3D.swf"
      width="640" height="400"
      debugMode="true" registerWithJS="true" xmlData="${strXML}" />
    </body>
</html>
```

3. Run this project from within Eclipse, and you should see the chart in your browser.

What just happened?

You just created a data-driven chart in Java. Let us explore how we did it.

In `ArrayExample.jsp`, we first included the FusionCharts tag library using the following code:

```
<%@ taglib prefix="c" uri="http://java.sun.com/jsp/jstl/core"%>
<%@ taglib prefix="tags" tagdir="/WEB-INF/tags"%>
<%@ taglib uri="http://www.fusioncharts.com/jsp/core" prefix="fc"%>
```

We then included `FusionCharts.js`, which is necessary to render the charts, by adding the following line of code:

```
<script src="Charts/FusionCharts.js"></script>
```

Next, we created an array to store the data for this chart. We store data for two categories of items—Food Products and Non-Food Products for three years, using the following code:

```
String[][] arrData = new String [3][3];
arrData[0][0] = "2009";
arrData[1][0] = "2010";
arrData[2][0] = "2011";
arrData[0][1] = "892500";
arrData[1][1] = "815300";
arrData[2][1] = "1407400";
arrData[0][2] = "595000";
arrData[1][2] = "693200";
arrData[2][2] = "880400";
```

Next is the most crucial part where we convert this data into XML. To do so, we create a string called `xmlData` and initialize it with the `<chart>` element and the requisite attributes for this chart:

```
String xmlData = "<chart caption='Break-up of sales for last 3 years'
  numberPrefix='$'>";
```

To add the x-axis labels, we need to create the `<categories>` and `<category>` elements, which is done using the following code. In this code, we iterate through our array and add 2009, 2010, and 2011 as the x-axis labels.

```
xmlData +=  " <categories> ";
for (int i = 0; i <= 2; i++) {
  xmlData += " <category label ='" + arrData[i][0] + "'/> ";
}
xmlData += "</categories>";
```

Thereafter, we add the XML element `<dataset>` for two data series, namely Food Products and Non-Food Products, and also the data points under each data series as a `<set>` element. To do this, we iterate through our array again, using the following lines of code:

```
xmlData += "<dataset seriesName='Sales of Food Products'>";
for(int i = 0; i <= 2; i++) {
  xmlData += "<set value = '" + arrData[i][1] + "'/>";
}
xmlData += "</dataset>";
xmlData += "<dataset seriesName='Sales of Non-Food Products'>";
for(int i = 0; i <= 2; i++) {
  xmlData += "<set value = '" + arrData[i][1] + "'/>";
}
xmlData += "</dataset>";
```

Finally, we append the closing `</chart>` element to the string variable. If, at this point in time, you have seen the contents of `xmlData`, you will have seen the entire XML for our multi-series chart.

The only thing left is to embed the chart in the page, for which we make use of the FusionCharts tag library, instead of writing direct JavaScript code.

```
<c:set var="strXML" value="<%=xmlData%>" />
test:${strXML}
<fc:render chartId="chart_from_array"
  swfFilename="Charts/MSColumn3D.swf"
  width="640" height="400"
  debugMode="true" registerWithJS="true" xmlData="${strXML}" />
```

Here, we are creating a multi-series Column 3D chart, whose SWF is `MSColumn3D.swf`, giving it an ID of `chart_from_array`, a width of 600 and height of 400. We are also relaying the XML data we earlier created in `xmlData` to this chart using the Data String method. This method internally generates the complete JavaScript and HTML code to add the chart to the page.

What if you wished to render the chart as JavaScript, or provide data in JSON?

When rendering FusionCharts in Java using the FusionCharts tag library, you can choose to render the chart in JavaScript only, by adding the `renderer` attribute, as in the following code:

```
<fc:render chartId="${chartData.chartId}"
    swfFilename="${folderPath}${chartData.
swfFilename}"
    width="${chartData.width}" height="${chartData.
height}"
    debugMode="false" registerWithJS="true"
    xmlUrl="${chartData.url}" renderer="javascript"/>
```

Similarly, to provide JSON data to the chart, instead of XML, you can use the `jsonURL` attribute, instead of `xmlUrl`, as in the following code:

```
<fc:render chartId="${chartData.chartId}"
    swfFilename="${folderPath}${chartData.
swfFilename}"
    width="${chartData.width}" height="${chartData.
height}"
    debugMode="false" registerWithJS="false"
    jsonUrl="${chartData.jsonUrl}" />
```

Now that we know the basics of how to create a dynamic chart, let's explore how to change the datasource from an array to a database. We will use the table `orders` that we created earlier. Using the data from this table, we will create a chart that lets Harry compare the annual revenues for the last three years.

Time for action – creating a chart in Java using data from MySQL

1. Create a new JSP file and save it as `AnnualRevenues.jsp`.

2. Paste the following code in it:

```
<!DOCTYPE HTML PUBLIC "-//W3C//DTD HTML 4.01 Transitional//EN"
    "http://www.w3.org/TR/html4/loose.dtd">
<%@ taglib prefix="c" uri="http://java.sun.com/jsp/jstl/core"%>
<%@ taglib prefix="tags" tagdir="/WEB-INF/tags"%>
<%@ taglib uri="http://www.fusioncharts.com/jsp/core"
    prefix="fc"%>
<%@ page import="java.sql.*" %>
<%@ page import="java.io.*" %>
<html>
  <head>
    <title>Database example in Java</title>
    <script type="text/javascript"
```

```
            src="FusionCharts/FusionCharts.js"></script>
    </head>
    <body>
      <h1>Creating charts in Java using data from MySQL</h1>
      <%
        try {
          String connectionURL =
            "jdbc:mysql://localhost:3306/harrys_supermarket";
          Connection connection = null;
          ResultSet rst=null;
          Statement stmt=null;
          Class.forName("com.mysql.jdbc.Driver").newInstance();
          connection = DriverManager.getConnection(connectionURL,
            "root", "root_pass");
          stmt=connection.createStatement();
          rst=stmt.executeQuery("SELECT SUM( order_amount ) AS SUM,
            YEAR( order_date ) AS YEAR FROM orders GROUP BY YEAR(
            order_date )");
          String strXML = "<chart caption='Annual Revenue - last 3
            years' numberPrefix='$'>";
          while(rst.next()){
            String year = rst.getString("YEAR");
            String total = rst.getString("SUM");
            strXML += "<set label = '"+year+"' value = '"+total+"'
              />";
          }
          strXML += "</chart>";
        %>
        <c:set var="strXML" value="<%=strXML%>" />
        <%
          rst.close();
          stmt.close();
          connection.close();
        }
        catch(Exception ex){
          out.println("Unable to connect to database.");
        }
      %>
      <fc:render chartId="annual_revenue"
        swfFilename="FusionCharts/Column3D.swf"
        width="640" height="400"debugMode="false"
        registerWithJS="true" xmlData="${strXML}" />
    </body>
</html>
```

3. Now, when you run the project, you should see a chart showing the annual revenues for the last three years, as we had seen earlier.

What just happened?

You just created a dynamic chart in Java by pulling in data from a MySQL database. Let's understand the code further.

In `AnnualRevenues.jsp`, we first included the FusionCharts tab library.

```
<%@ taglib prefix="c" uri="http://java.sun.com/jsp/jstl/core"%>
<%@ taglib prefix="tags" tagdir="/WEB-INF/tags"%>
<%@ taglib uri="http://www.fusioncharts.com/jsp/core" prefix="fc"%>
```

We also import the tab libraries to be able to connect to the database.

```
<%@ page import="java.sql.*" %>
<%@ page import="java.io.*" %>
```

Next, we include `FusionCharts.js`, required to render the charts in the page.

Thereafter, we connect to the database and execute the SQL query that returns the annual revenue for the last three years.

```
String connectionURL =
  "jdbc:mysql://localhost:3306/harrys_supermarket";
Connection connection = null;
ResultSet rst=null;
Statement stmt=null;
Class.forName("com.mysql.jdbc.Driver").newInstance();
connection = DriverManager.getConnection(connectionURL, "root",
  "root_pass");
stmt=connection.createStatement();
rst=stmt.executeQuery("SELECT SUM( order_amount ) AS SUM, YEAR(
  order_date ) AS YEAR FROM orders GROUP BY YEAR( order_date )");
```

When executing this code on your machine, be sure to replace the database credentials with your own.

Now that we have the recordset, we convert it into FusionCharts XML format. We initialize a string variable `strXML` that will contain XML for the chart and initialize the `<chart>` element.

```
String strXML = "<chart caption='Annual Revenue - last 3 years'
  numberPrefix='$'>";
```

To convert the data in the recordset to the FusionCharts XML format, we iterate through the recordset to add the `<set>` elements for the chart.

```
while(rst.next()){
  String year = rst.getString("YEAR");
  String total = rst.getString("SUM");
  strXML += "<set label = '"+year+"' value = '"+total+"' />";
}
strXML += "</chart>";
```

With the XML now ready in `strXML`, we render the chart using the FusionCharts tag library, using the following code:

```
<fc:render chartId="annual_revenue"
  swfFilename="FusionCharts/Column3D.swf"
  width="640" height="400"
  debugMode="false" registerWithJS="true" xmlData="${strXML}" />
```

Let us now add drill-down to the example that we just built, so that when Harry clicks on a year's column, he can see the quarterly sales for that year.

Time for action – creating a drill-down chart in Java using data from MySQL

1. In `AnnualRevenues.jsp`, modify this line of code:

```
strXML += "<set label = '"+year+"' value = '"+total+"' link =
  'Quarterly.jsp?year="+year+"'/>";
```

2. And this line as well:

```
String strXML = "<chart caption='Annual Revenue - last 3 years'
  subcaption='Click on a column to view revenue for each quarter
  for that year' numberPrefix='$'>";
```

3. Add another file to this project and name it as `Quarterly.jsp`.

4. Paste the following code in it:

```
<!DOCTYPE HTML PUBLIC "-//W3C//DTD HTML 4.01 Transitional//EN"
  "http://www.w3.org/TR/html4/loose.dtd">
<%@ taglib prefix="c" uri="http://java.sun.com/jsp/jstl/core"%>
<%@ taglib prefix="tags" tagdir="/WEB-INF/tags"%>
<%@ taglib uri="http://www.fusioncharts.com/jsp/core"
  prefix="fc"%>
<%@ page import="java.sql.*" %>
<%@ page import="java.io.*" %>
<html>
```

```
<head>
  <title>Quarterly revenues</title>
  <script type="text/javascript"
    src="FusionCharts/FusionCharts.js"></script>
</head>
<body>
  <h1>Drill-down Charts in Java</h1>
  <%
    try {
      String connectionURL =
        "jdbc:mysql://localhost:3306/harrys_supermarket";
      Connection connection = null;
      ResultSet rst=null;
      Statement stmt=null;
      Class.forName("com.mysql.jdbc.Driver").newInstance();
      connection = DriverManager.getConnection(connectionURL,
        "root", "root_pass");
      String year = request.getParameter("year");
      stmt=connection.createStatement();
      rst=stmt.executeQuery("SELECT SUM(order_amount) AS SUM,
        QUARTER(order_date) AS Quarter FROM orders WHERE
        YEAR(order_date) = " + year + " AND
        QUARTER(order_date) IN (SELECT QUARTER(order_date)
        FROM orders) GROUP BY Quarter");
      String strXML = "<chart caption='Quarterly Revenue -
        '"+year+"' numberPrefix='$'>";
      while(rst.next()){
        String quarter = rst.getString("Quarter");
        String total = rst.getString("SUM");
        strXML += "<set label = 'Qtr - "+quarter+"' value =
          '"+total+"' />";
      }
      strXML += "</chart>";
    %>
    <c:set var="strXML" value="<%=strXML%>" />
    <%
      rst.close();
      stmt.close();
      connection.close();
    }
    catch(Exception ex){
      out.println("Unable to connect to database.");
    }
  %>
  <fc:render chartId="quarterly_revenue"
```

```
        swfFilename="FusionCharts/Column3D.swf" width="640"
        height="400"debugMode="false" registerWithJS="true"
        xmlData="${strXML}" />
    </body>
</html>
```

5. Save the changes and run the project from Eclipse. The first page should show a chart with the annual revenues. But this time, when you click on any column of any year, the chart should drill-down to show the quarterly revenue.

What just happened?

We enabled drill-down on the annual revenues chart, whose column when clicked takes us to another page showing the quarterly revenues for a particular year.

To add drill-down to the first chart contained in `AnnualRevenues.jsp`, we added the `link` attribute to the `<set>` elements.

```
strXML += "<set label = '"+year+"' value = '"+total+"' link =
    'Quarterly.jsp?year="+year+"'/>";
```

The link points to the file `Quarterly.jsp` that we just created. We also pass the value of each year as a QueryString to this page. The `<set>` element for 2009 would look similar to the following line of code, once generated:

```
<set label='2009' value=' 1487500 link='Quarterly.jsp?year=2009' />
```

As a good practice, we also inform the users that the chart supports drill-down by adding information to the chart's subcaption.

```
String strXML = "<chart caption='Annual Revenue - last 3 years'
    subcaption='Click on a column to view revenue for each quarter for
    that year' numberPrefix='$'>";
```

Now, we need to create the quarterly chart in `Quarterly.jsp`. To do this, we request the year for which we've to plot the quarterly chart. This year was passed to the page as a QueryString with the key `year` from the page `AnnualRevenues.aspx`. Whenever a user clicks on a column, the link invoked contains the year as the QueryString.

```
String year = request.getParameter("year");
```

We then connect to the database and get the quarterly revenues for the year as present in the database.

```
Class.forName("com.mysql.jdbc.Driver").newInstance();
connection = DriverManager.getConnection(connectionURL, "root",
  "root_pass");
String year = request.getParameter("year");
stmt=connection.createStatement();
rst=stmt.executeQuery("SELECT SUM(order_amount) AS SUM,
  QUARTER(order_date) AS Quarter FROM orders WHERE YEAR(order_date) =
  " + year + " AND QUARTER(order_date) IN (SELECT QUARTER(order_date)
  FROM orders) GROUP BY Quarter");
```

Next, we convert the recordset to XML by iterating through it, as earlier, using the following lines of code:

```
String strXML = "<chart caption='Quarterly Revenue - '"+year+"'
  numberPrefix='$'>";
while(rst.next()){
  String quarter = rst.getString("Quarter");
  String total = rst.getString("SUM");
  strXML += "<set label = 'Qtr - "+quarter+"' value = '"+total+"'
    />";
}
strXML += "</chart>";
```

Finally, we render the chart, using the following code:

```
<fc:render chartId="quarterly_revenue"
  swfFilename="FusionCharts/Column3D.swf"width="640" height="400"
  debugMode="false" registerWithJS="true" xmlData="${strXML}" />
```

And this completes the drill-down example in Java. You are now equipped to build multi-level dashboards using FusionCharts, with a variety of chart combinations in each page.

Have a go hero – build a dashboard for Harry

Extend our previous example to add another level of drill-down for Harry, so that he can click on any quarter to explore monthly sales data.

instead of opening each child chart in a new page, use the LinkedCharts feature of FusionCharts to allow opening in lightboxes.

Summary

In this chapter, we learned how to connect FusionCharts to the server-side script to build charts using dynamic data. We created drill-down charts in PHP, ASP.NET, and Java, and understood the real-world use cases of database-driven drill-down charts. You can use the same concepts of integration with any other server-side scripts such as Python, Ruby on Rails, ColdFusion, and so on.

In the next chapter, we will learn how to create data-driven maps that can use geographical data.

7
Creating Maps for your Applications

Harry's grip on his business is better than ever before. He is able to compare his revenue over time and identify trends, thanks to the charts we have created for him. Now, he wants to find the answer to another question—which states are generating good revenue for me and which ones are doing poorly? Given that his online presence spans a lot more of the US as opposed to his smaller brick-and-mortar presence, this is a critical business question for him. And of course, for questions like this, geography plays a big part and it is best visualized on a map. Time to say hello to FusionMaps , a part of FusionCharts Suite.

FusionMaps helps you display geographical data distributed by regions or entities using animated and interactive maps. You can use it to plot business data such as revenue by regions, census data such as population by state, and election results, effectively. In this chapter, we will use FusionMaps to let Harry know which states are doing well and which ones are not, by color coding them.

In this chapter, you will learn how to:

- ◆ Download and set up FusionMaps
- ◆ Create a simple map to plot Harry's online revenue
- ◆ Configure the map to use your own regional identifiers as opposed to the preset ones
- ◆ Build a map for Harry that lets him drill down from the US map to different states

Getting FusionMaps

In *Chapter 1*, *Introducing FusionCharts*, we got ourselves an evaluation copy of FusionCharts XT. Similar to the charts, you can download a no-restriction trial version of FusionMaps as well from the FusionCharts website. The installation procedure is similar too, and we will see how to do it next up.

Time for action – downloading and extracting FusionMaps

1. Go to http://www.fusioncharts.com/download and fill in your particulars in the download form.

2. After filling in your details, click on the download link for FusionMaps.

3. Once the ZIP has been downloaded, extract it to a folder on your hard-drive, C:\FusionChartsSuite\FusionMaps or Users/{YourName}/FusionChartsSuite/FusionMaps. We will refer to this folder as **FusionMaps Installation Folder**.

What just happened?

You have now successfully downloaded FusionMaps and extracted it in the FusionMaps Installation Folder. The folder structure is very similar to the FusionCharts XT package with the map SWF files present in the Maps folder. The only difference is that the JavaScript class to embed the map in your web page is present in a separate JSClass folder.

The Maps folder contains 315 maps including all continents, major countries, and US states. Additionally, Europe, America, and India maps can be downloaded by licensed users from the Product Update Center at www.fusioncharts.com/PUC, thus offering a total of over 550 maps. To explore the maps locally, open Index.html, which opens up the documentation. Head to **Map Gallery** using the menu on the left, and click on the map you would like to explore.

As you can see, each map is divided into regions, for which you can set values using their **preset identifiers**. To see these identifiers, just head to **Map Specification Sheets** in the documentation and find the map you are looking for. The following screenshot displays the **World Map Specification Sheet**:

World Map Specification Sheet

Map Name: World Map
SWF Name: FCMap_World.swf
Dimensions (Width x Height): 750 x 400 pixels
Selection: Continents

List of Entities

Internal Id	Short Name (Abbreviated Name)	Long Name
NA	NA	North America
SA	SA	South America
EU	EU	Europe
AF	AF	Africa
AU	AU	Australia
AS	AS	Asia

The sheet has three columns, **Internal ID**, **Short Name**, and **Long Name**. The Internal ID is the predefined ID for each region in the map that we use to define data in the XML file. The **Short Name** is the name that appears on the map for the region and the **Long Name** in the tooltip. For each map you create, you will be making use of the respective map specification sheet.

Creating the first map

For our first map, we will be plotting the online revenue Harry makes from different states in the US. The following table lists the data for the 10 states Harry sells to online, for which we will be plotting:

State	Revenue
Alabama	78000
California	148000
Florida	95100
Hawaii	77000
Illinois	21000
Louisiana	128000
Massachusetts	50000
Nevada	93000
New York	128000
Texas	38000

We will be using different color codes to mark out the performance as good, average, and bad. The ranges that Harry has decided are in the following table:

Range	Name	Color
0-20000	Poor	FF9377 (Red)
20000-30000	Average	FFFFCC (Yellow)
30000-100000	Good	A7E9BC (Green)

Technically, there are three steps to creating a map:

◆ Finding the appropriate map for the region in the Maps folder

◆ Creating the XML data for the map

◆ Writing the HTML and JavaScript code to embed the map in the page

Time for action – set up FusionMaps for our first map

1. Create a folder called FusionMaps under the LearningFusionCharts folder. This folder will contain all the SWF and JavaScript files of FusionMaps, which are the **FusionMaps Core Files**. If you are working on a web server, create this folder under the root of the web application, so that the entire web application can conveniently access this.

2. For the sake of ease, copy and paste all the SWF files from your FusionMaps Installation Folder (the place where you had earlier downloaded and extracted the FusionMaps ZIP file) | Maps to the newly created FusionMaps folder.

3. Copy and paste FusionMaps.js from FusionMaps Installation Folder | JSClass to the FusionMaps folder.

4. Create another folder under LearningFusionCharts and name it as LearningFusionMaps. This will be used to store XML data and HTML files for all the maps we create in this chapter.

What just happened?

You just installed FusionMaps and are ready to use any of the maps available in it for your application. Typically, in any application, you will be plotting only a subset of the maps available, so you can select only those SWF files and paste them here. However, copying all files makes it easier in the future whenever you need to create the map of a new region. We also pasted the FusionMaps.js file which is the **FusionMaps JavaScript class**. This class helps you embed maps in your HTML page in a more user-friendly way and helps avoid the Internet Explorer **Click to Activate this control** issue.

With the installation done, we are now ready to create the XML data for Harry's state-wise revenue chart.

Time for action – creating the XML for our first map

1. Create an empty XML file in the `LearningFusionMaps` folder and name it as `Data.xml`.

2. Write the following XML in the file and save it:

```
<map fillColor='F1F1F1' numberPrefix='$'>
  <colorRange>
    <color minValue='0' maxValue='40000' displayValue='Poor'
      color='FF9377' />
    <color minValue='40000' maxValue='100000'
      displayValue='Average' color='FFFFCC' />
    <color minValue='100000' maxValue='5000000'
      displayValue='Good' color='A7E9BC' />
  </colorRange>
  <data>
    <entity id='AL' value='78000' />
    <entity id='CA' value='148000' />
    <entity id='FL' value='95100' />
    <entity id='HI' value='77000' />
    <entity id='IL' value='21000' />
    <entity id='LA' value='128000' />
    <entity id='MA' value='50000' />
    <entity id='NV' value='93000' />
    <entity id='NY' value='128000' />
    <entity id='TX' value='38000' />
  </data>
</map>
```

What just happened?

We just defined the data for our first map. To start with, the XML for each map you create has to have the `<map>` element. Similar to the charts, the attributes of the map give you control over both the functional and cosmetic properties of the map. For our map, we defined the default fill for the entities using the `fillColor` attribute. This color will be shown for all the states that we are not plotting values for; the other states will pick up colors depending on which range they fall in. We also prefixed $ to the numbers on the chart using the `numberPrefix` attribute.

To define the color range, we use the `<colorRange>...</colorRange>` elements. Each color range thereafter is defined using the `<color>` element for which we have specified its starting value, ending value, name, and color, as in the following lines of code:

```
<colorRange>
  <color minValue='0' maxValue='40000' displayValue='Poor'
    color='FF9377' />
  <color minValue='40000' maxValue='100000' displayValue='Average'
    color='FFFFCC' />
  <color minValue='100000' maxValue='5000000' displayValue='Good'
    color='A7E9BC' />
</colorRange>
```

Then begins the actual data for the chart enclosed within the `<data>` and `</data>` elements. For each state that we want to plot a value for, we need the `<entity>` element. Then, using the ID of the state from the specification sheet (**Map Specification Sheets | USA & States | USA**), we associate values to them, as in the following line of code:

```
<entity id='AL' value='78000' />
```

Time for action – writing the HTML and the JavaScript code to embed the map in a page

1. Create a new file called `FirstMap.html` under the `LearningFusionMaps` folder.

2. Write the following code in the page and save it:

```html
<html>
  <head>
    <title>My First Map</title>
    <script language="JavaScript"
      src="../FusionMaps/FusionMaps.js"></script>
  </head>
  <body>
    <div id="mapdiv" align="center">
      FusionMaps.
    </div>
    <script type="text/javascript">
      var map = new FusionMaps("../FusionMaps/FCMap_USA.swf",
        "Map1Id", "750", "400", "0", "0");
      map.setDataURL("Data.xml");
      map.render("mapdiv");
    </script>
  </body>
</html>
```

3. Open the HTML file in a browser to see your first map in action.

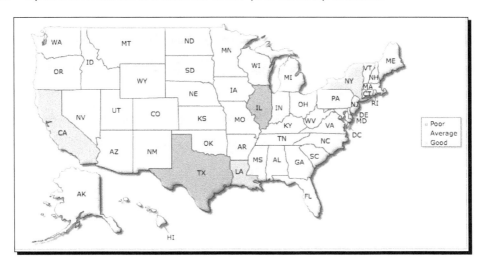

What just happened?

You just created your first map. The HTML code is very similar to what we have been using to create charts.

First up, we included the FusionMaps JavaScript class in the same way we included `FusionCharts.js` earlier:

```
<script language="JavaScript"
  src="../FusionMaps/FusionMaps.js"></script>
```

Then we created a `<div>` to render the map in, and initialized the map by invoking the **FusionMaps JavaScript constructor**.

```
var map = new FusionMaps("../FusionMaps/FCMap_USA.swf", "Map1Id",
  "750", "400", "0", "1");
```

The parameters it accepts are the same as that for the chart:

- The path and filename of the map SWF
- The ID of the map
- The width and height of the map
- Settings for `debugMode` and `registerWithJS`, the latter being a legacy parameter that is now mandatorily set to `1`, as the maps are tightly integrated with JavaScript

Yes, that's how easy it is to go about creating your own interactive maps for your application.

Have a go hero – remove the "3D" effect of the map

By default, all the maps in FusionMaps have a bevel and shadow effect that give them a 3D look. However, many applications need the map to be flat to go along with the feel of the rest of the application. Using the attributes specified in the documentation at **FusionMaps and XML | XML Attributes**, remove both these effects to render the map in plain 2D.

Defining new IDs for the entities

Picture this: Harry has internal ERP where he has his own three-letter internal codes for all the states as in the following table:

State	ID in ERP	FusionMaps ID	Revenue
Alabama	ALB	AL	78000
California	CLF	CA	148000
Florida	FLR	FL	95100
Hawaii	HWI	HI	77000
Illinois	ILL	IL	21000
Louisiana	LOU	LA	128000
Massachusetts	MAS	MA	50000
Nevada	NVD	NV	93000
New York	NWY	NY	128000
Texas	TXS	TX	38000

If you provide data to FusionMaps using the IDs stored in the ERP, it will refuse to identify them. FusionMaps only understands the preset IDs present in the map specification sheet of the region. Checking and converting each of these IDs into the preset ones every single time involves a lot of manual effort. And, if you have to manually map the internal ID to FusionMaps ID, each time the XML has to be generated using the `if-then` clause, it will be time consuming. FusionMaps has a simpler way to take care of this – you can redefine the entity IDs at once along with the short and the long name. The XML data will look similar to the following lines of code with entity redefinitions:

```
<map fillColor='F1F1F1' numberPrefix='$'>
  <colorRange>
    <color minValue='0' maxValue='40000' displayValue='Poor'
      color='FF9377' />
    <color minValue='40000' maxValue='100000' displayValue='Average'
      color='FFFFCC' />
    <color minValue='100000' maxValue='5000000' displayValue='Good'
      color='A7E9BC' />
```

```
    </colorRange>
    <entityDef>
      <entity internalId='AL' newId='ALB' sName='ALBM' lName='Alabama
        State'/>
      <entity internalId='CA' newId='CLF' sName='CLFA'
        lName='California State'/>
      <entity internalId='FL' newId='FLR' sName='FLRD' lName='Florida
        State'/>
      <entity internalId='HI' newId='HWI' sName='HWII' lName='Hawaii
        State'/>
      <entity internalId='IL' newId='ILL' sName='ILLI' lName='Illinois
        State'/>
      <entity internalId='LA' newId='LOU' sName='LOUI' lName='Louisiana
        State'/>
      <entity internalId='MA' newId='MAS' sName='MASS'
        lName='Massachusetts State'/>
      <entity internalId='NV' newId='NVD' sName='NVDA' lName='Nevada
        State'/>
      <entity internalId='NY' newId='NWY' sName='NWYK' lName='New York
        State'/>
      <entity internalId='TX' newId='TXS' sName='TXAS' lName='Texas
        State'/>
    </entityDef>
    <data>
      <entity id='ALB' value='78000' />
      <entity id='CLF' value='148000' />
      <entity id='FLR' value='95100' />
      <entity id='HWI' value='77000' />
      <entity id='ILL' value='21000' />
      <entity id='LOU' value='128000' />
      <entity id='MAS' value='50000' />
      <entity id='NVD' value='93000' />
      <entity id='NWY' value='128000' />
      <entity id='TXS' value='38000' />
    </data>
  </map>
```

As you can see, new entity definitions have to be enclosed within the `<entityDef>` and `</entityDef>` elements. For each entity that we need to redefine the ID for, we use the `<entity>` element, the `internalId` attribute helps us refer to the entity using its preset ID and, `newId` helps us define the new ID according to the ERP. Also, to change the short and the long name, we use the `sName` and `lName` attributes respectively. That's it! We can now refer to these states using the IDs we have in the ERP instead of the preset ones in FusionMaps. You must remember that the regions cannot be referred to using their old preset IDs in the `<entity>` element, they have to use the new ID.

Creating drill-down maps

Harry has tasted blood and is getting more demanding now. The map we created gives him a very good idea of which state is doing well, and now he wants to be able to drill down to the state map to see how the counties in there are doing.

Time for action – drilling down from the US map to the individual states

1. Create a folder called `DrillDown` under `LearningFusionMaps`, where we will store the HTML and XML files for both the parent US map and the 10 state maps it drills down to.

2. Make a copy of `FirstMap.html` and `Data.xml` under the `DrillDown` folder, and rename them as `DrillDown.html` and `DrillDown.xml` respectively.

3. Update the relative path of the FusionMaps JavaScript class and the US map in `DrillDown.html` using the following lines of code:

```
<script language="JavaScript"
  src="../../FusionMaps/FusionMaps.js"></script>
var map = new FusionMaps("../../FusionMaps/FCMap_USA.swf",
  "Map1Id", "750", "400", "0", "1");
```

4. Change the URL of the XML file in `DrillDown.html` to the new file as well, using the following line of code:

```
map.setDataURL("DrillDown.xml");
```

5. Create an XML file `Alabama.xml` in the `DrillDown` folder with the following data:

```
<map fillColor='F1F1F1' numberPrefix='$'>
  <colorRange>
    <color minValue='0' maxValue='10000' displayValue='Poor'
      color='FF9377' />
    <color minValue='10000' maxValue='20000'
      displayValue='Average' color='FFFFCC' />
    <color minValue='20000' maxValue='1000000' displayValue='Good'
      color='A7E9BC' />
  </colorRange>
  <data>
    <entity id='001' value='20000' />
    <entity id='005' value='16000' />
    <entity id='021' value='7000' />
    <entity id='029' value='35000' />
  </data>
</map>
```

6. Create an HTML file `Alabama.html` and type the following code in it:

```html
<html>
  <head>
    <title>My First Map</title>
    <script language="JavaScript"
      src="../../FusionMaps/FusionMaps.js"></script>
  </head>
  <body>
    <div id="mapdiv" align="center">
      FusionMaps.
    </div>
    <script type="text/javascript">
      var map =
      new FusionMaps("../../FusionMaps/FCMap_Alabama.swf",
      "Map1Id", "475","575", "0", "1");
      map.setDataURL("Alabama.xml");
      map.render("mapdiv");
    </script>
    <center><a href='DrillDown.html'>Back to US Map</a></center>
  </body>
</html>
```

7. Similarly, create the XML and HTML files for all the other states as well using the convention `{StateName}.xml` and `{StateName}.html`. The entire code is available as a part of the download package of the book, and is not repeated here for brevity.

8. Now, in `DrillDown.xml`, link each of the states to the respective state maps, using the following lines of code:

```xml
<map fillColor='F1F1F1' numberPrefix='$'>
  <colorRange>
    <color minValue='0' maxValue='40000' displayValue='Poor'
      color='FF9377' />
    <color minValue='40000' maxValue='100000'
      displayValue='Average' color='FFFFCC' />
    <color minValue='100000' maxValue='5000000'
      displayValue='Good' color='A7E9BC' />
  </colorRange>
  <data>
    <entity id='AL' value='78000' link='Alabama.html'/>
    <entity id='CA' value='148000' link='California.html'/>
    <entity id='FL' value='95100' link='Florida.html'/>
    <entity id='HI' value='77000' link='Hawaii.html'/>
    <entity id='IL' value='21000' link='Illinois.html'/>
```

```
      <entity id='LA' value='128000' link='Louisiana.html'/>
      <entity id='MA' value='50000' link='Massachusetts.html'/>
      <entity id='NV' value='93000' link='Nevada.html'/>
      <entity id='NY' value='128000' link='NewYork.html'/>
      <entity id='TX' value='38000' link='Texas.html'/>
   </data>
</map>
```

9. Open `DrillDown.html` in a browser and click on any of the states, say Alabama, to drill down into the state map, as shown in the following screenshot:

What just happened?

We first created the HTML and XML files for the parent map in the `DrillDown` folder. Then we created the HTML and XML files for all the state maps showing the breakdown of the revenue in the state. Once that was done, it was a simple matter of linking each state to its respective state map using the `link` attribute of the `<entity>` element in the parent map.

```
<entity id='AL' value='78000' link='Alabama.html'/>
```

Similar to the charts, the drill-down opens in a new window, a frame, a pop up window, and even invokes JavaScript functions just like we discussed in *Chapter 4, Enabling Drill-down on Charts*.

Have a go hero – drill-down from the map to a chart

Until now, we have created charts drilling down to more detailed charts, and maps drilling down to more detailed maps. In business reports and dashboards, you will often need to have a drill-down from a map to a chart or the other way round. Facilitate one of these cases by having a drill-down from the US map to a pie chart showing the category-wise breakdown of the items sold in the state. Choose the categories as you prefer—apparels, electronics, household items, and so on.

Summary

In this chapter, we learned how to create maps to display region-based geographical data. The maps are used in executive dashboards to display business data such as revenue by regions, census data such as population by state, and election results, effectively.

Specifically we covered:

◆ How to create a simple map with range-based data having appropriate color codes

◆ How to map the IDs of entities stored in your internal system or database to the ones preset in FusionMaps

◆ How to create drill-down from one map to another, say continent to country or country to state

In the next chapter, we will see how to select the right chart type for the data we have and the analysis we want to facilitate.

8
Selecting the Right Visualization for your Data

We have done a good job of converting all the data Harry wanted to see into beautiful and quick-to-understand visuals. The charts and maps have helped Harry get a lot of insights out of information that would have been difficult from the raw data itself.

As you build complete business dashboards catering to different people in the organization, you will need to understand their role and function better. For example, Harry will be interested in the overall company stats such as annual revenue and market share, while a regional manager will be interested in the revenue and the best selling product categories from his own region. Once you have identified the metrics your audience needs, you need to figure the data required to power the metric, and then select the right visualization for it.

In this chapter, we shall learn:

- ◆ How to adapt the dashboard according to the requirement of its audience
- ◆ What type of analysis the metrics identified require and the chart needed for it
- ◆ How to use specialized charts such as Gauges and Gantt charts used for advanced analysis

So let's get started.

Understanding the audience

At Harry's SuperMart, the metrics that different people in the organization look at will vary depending on their roles and responsibilities.

For Harry, the CEO, the important metrics would be the revenue trends as compared to earlier years, comparisons with the overall market and important competitors, best and worst performing product categories, spend across various functions of the company, and overall customer satisfaction.

However, a regional manager reporting to Harry would look at more detailed data such as the year-to-date revenue coming from his region, the contribution of his region to overall revenue, and inventory levels in the region.

Similarly, a store manager who reports to a regional manager will look at the average sale per customer coming to the store, the breakdown of new and returning customers, daily footfall, the attendance levels of his employees, and his current inventory levels in the store.

Broadly, the dashboard audience can be classified under the following three headings:

◆ **Strategic users**: This includes the board of directors, management, and key executives of an organization. strategic users look at all aspects of the organization from a very high-level perspective without focusing on the day-to-day details. Their aim is to align the business with overall strategic objectives and look at the long-term picture. As such, dashboards for strategic users contain mostly historical data without the need for any real-time data.

◆ **Tactical users**: This includes department managers, business analysts, and other mid-level managers. These users look at the performance of their own department, which is just one of the aspects of a strategic dashboard, and compare it with the organization's performance to look for areas of concern. The metrics for tactical users may need real-time data.

◆ **Operational users**: This includes frontline workers and managers who deal directly with customers or manage production. These users look at real-time transactional-level data to continuously monitor their business processes, and receive an alert on any threshold value being exceeded.

Let's see how each of these users will look at the customer support function of an organization. The CEO, a strategic user, will just look at the overall customer satisfaction rating to understand how well his support department is doing. The customer support head, a tactical user, will look at the turnaround time, the number of tickets coming in on a monthly basis, the type of queries coming in, the percentage of queries that remain unresolved, and so on. A customer support executive, an operational user, will look at the number of tickets assigned to him, the number of tickets that he has answered on a given day, his turnaround time, and so on.

Typically, in an organization, the strategic dashboard cascades down to tactical and further to the operational dashboard with a good security model in place. In this way, everyone is aligned with the overall organizational goals but has access to no more data than required. However, standalone strategic, tactical, or operational dashboards are not uncommon in organizations and may be developed to focus on special aspects of the organization or important projects. In either case, the key is to understand the audience of the dashboard and identify the metrics that they will need to see. Once that is done, you need to figure out the kind of analysis you need to facilitate the selected metric and after that, it is a simple case of choosing the right visualization for the data.

Pop Quiz – know your dashboard audience

1. For which of the following types of users will your dashboard show the most high-level view of the organization?

    a. CEO

    b. Marketing Manager

    c. Field Sales Executive

Common types of data analysis

Different metrics need different kinds of analysis to get actionable information from the underlying data. There are certain metrics that can be analyzed from a couple of different angles. But once you know the business need for the metric, you will be able to figure out the data analysis needed easily.

Commonly, there are three types of data analysis that you will come across in day-to-day usage:

◆ Comparison of data

◆ Transition of data

◆ Composition of data

There are advanced charts that facilitate more than one analysis in the same chart that we will look at later in the chapter.

Comparison of data

Comparison analysis enables us to identify the highs and lows of data. For instance, by applying comparison analysis to the sales figures of 10 individuals, the best and the worst performers can easily be identified.

Comparison analysis is done with the help of column charts (also known as vertical bar charts) and bar charts. In these charts, data values are represented as columns and bars with lengths proportional to the respective values. So, in a dashboard for Harry's SuperMart, if Harry wanted to look at the monthly revenue for last year to identify the best and worst performing months, we would use a column chart, as shown in the following screenshot:

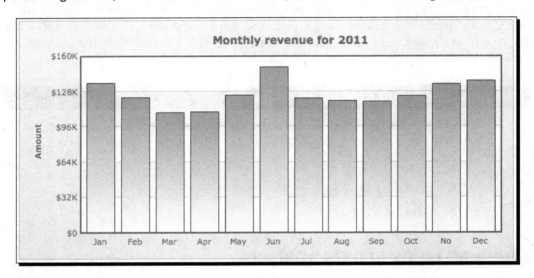

Using the column chart, Harry can easily see that June brought him the best revenue and March edged April to be the worst performing month.

Column and bar charts are very much alike in terms of core functionality, but they are meant for data with differing properties. The column chart is ideally used for representing data with short category descriptions and about 12-15 categories. The bar chart, on the other hand, is meant for displaying data with long category labels and a lot of categories. So, if a regional manager wanted to see the top 15 selling items in his region by revenue, we would need to use the bar chart.

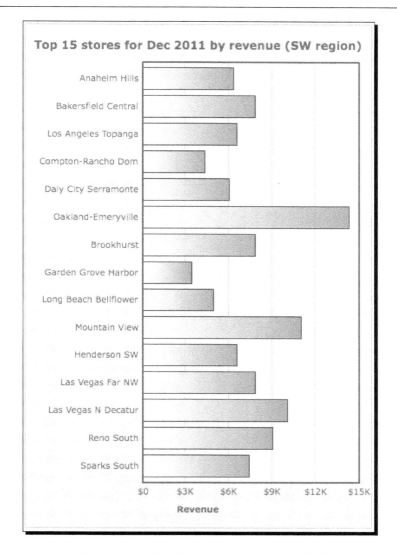

As you can see in the previous screenshot, bar charts are a better fit for long category labels as they are stacked on top of each other instead of being next to each other, as in the column chart.

An important point to note is that whenever your data does not have to follow a sequence (time or alphabetical), it is a good idea to arrange it in ascending or descending order. In the column chart, as the data is monthly, we cannot rearrange it. But in the bar chart, where there is no such order, we can arrange it in descending order for quicker understanding.

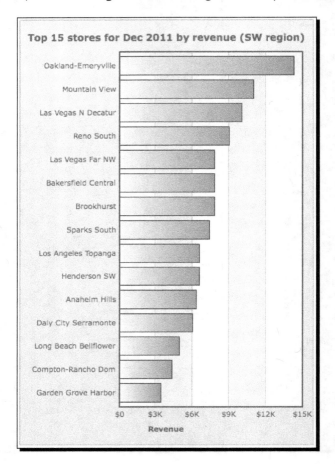

Transition of data

Transition analysis is applied to time-based data to understand the **trend of change**. For example, if you had to check whether the education levels in a state had been going up or down in the past decade, you would use transition analysis.

The line chart is the most commonly used chart for transition analysis. So if one of Harry's marketing managers had to see if daily website traffic had been going up or down as the month progressed, we would use the line chart.

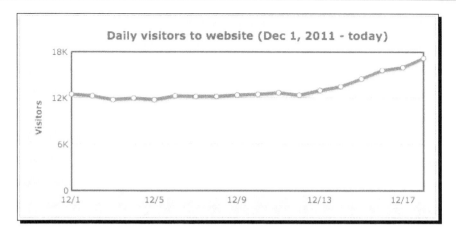

As the data points are connected to each other in a line chart, so it is easier for the human eye to follow them along and understand the trend of change as opposed to the column and bar chart, where each data point is a separate entity. Finding out the individual values of the data points with the line chart is not too difficult a task either. It is just that the columns and bars with lengths proportional to their values and direction parallel to the numeric axis, bring out the individual magnitudes better.

The area chart, which is very similar to the line chart, is also used for transition analysis. When used to plot a small set of data points, the area chart typically brings out the data better as the entire area is colored. Let us go ahead and plot the data from the previous line chart on an area chart.

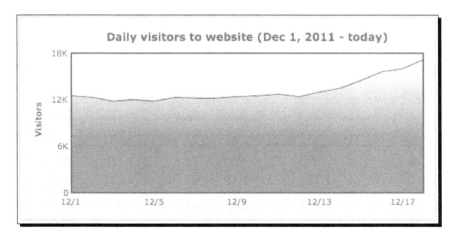

In this case, the area chart does a good job of bringing out the trend, as the number of data points is not too high. However, when used for plotting a lot of data points, especially with sudden spikes and falls, the resulting area chart will be "hard" on the eyes. Also for plotting multiple data series on the chart, the line chart is typically a cleaner pick. As a rule of thumb, whenever you are unsure of which chart to pick, just stick with the simpler line chart.

Composition of data

Composition analysis helps us understand how a data value breaks down into its constituents. For example, if you had to see the breakdown of the traffic to your website from various sources such as search, referring sites, and direct traffic, you would use composition analysis.

A pie chart is the most commonly used chart for analyzing the composition of data. So if Harry had to analyze how company revenue breaks down across different product categories, we would give him the pie chart, shown in the following screenshot:

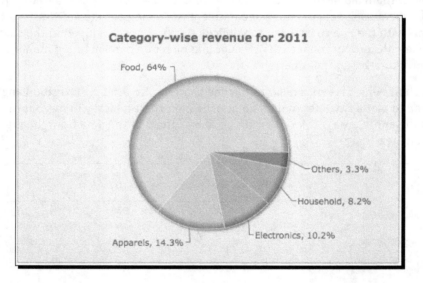

Quite clearly, selling food items gives Harry the maximum revenue, followed by apparels and electronics.

Composition analysis has another variation as well—a slightly more specialized one. Suppose one of Harry's store managers wanted to do an inventory audit of men's t-shirts in his outlet. At the start of the month, he will typically have some stock from the previous month. Some of these units may have been damaged while different people were seeing or trying them on. The manager can get his team to work on the damaged units and refurbish some of them. After all the subtractions and additions, we finally come to the number of salable units the manager has in hand at the beginning of the month. This kind of composition analysis is plotted with the help of a waterfall chart, which essentially is an advanced variant of a column chart. In the following screenshot, we see how the waterfall chart showing this analysis will look:

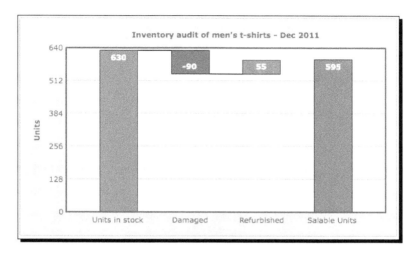

Combination of multiple forms of analysis

The common types of data analysis we have looked at till now are straightforward and will serve you well in most cases. Using the same principles, you can also plot multiple series of data in the comparison and transition charts. For example, in the column chart showing monthly revenue, you can have another series of columns plotting the values from last year, as shown in the following screenshot:

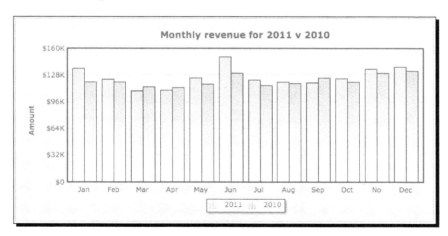

With data for 2010 as well, you can compare each month with last year's figures. But you would have noticed that comparing only the 2011 values has become a little tough, with the alternating 2010 values being a distraction. This is where the **interactive legend** comes into the picture. To hide all the values in the 2010 data series, just click on its icon in the legend, as shown in the following screenshot, and you can focus completely on the 2011 data series:

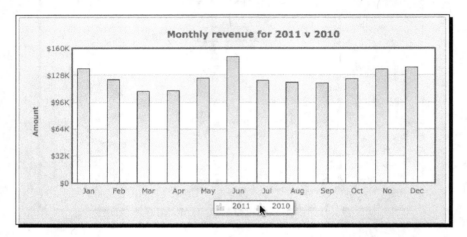

To bring the 2010 data series back into view, you just have to click on the icon again. However, if you want both the data series to be visible on the chart at all times, you will need to combine two different chart types as we will look at later.

The line chart can also add more context to the data by displaying the daily traffic stats for last month as well, as shown in the following screenshot:

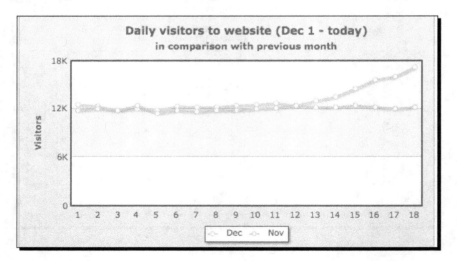

If the aim is to see the traffic trend for both the months individually, the previous line chart does the job perfectly. When analyzing the data, the two data series do not interfere with one another as in the column chart. The difference in traffic between the two months also comes out pretty well, but the column chart does a better job of it as we saw earlier.

Combination of comparison and transition charts

Both the column and the line chart we saw with two series of data have their own pros and cons. But if you know the kind of analysis you are trying to facilitate, making your pick is not difficult at all. Just like we plotted two series of data on the chart, you can go ahead and plot multiple series of data on the chart with the same principles holding true. This works fine until:

- ◆ You need to facilitate comparison analysis for a data series, and plot either predicted values, or the values of the previous year or month to add context to the data. In the monthly revenue column chart with data for 2010 and 2011, we saw how the chart facilitates comparison between Jan 2011 and Jan 2010 better but hinders comparative analysis for 2011 as a whole. The website traffic line chart on the other hand brings out the trend of both November and December well but gives only an indicative idea of the difference in traffic between say Nov 1 and Dec 1.

- ◆ The series use different units. For example, in a chart showing the revenue from a particular product category, if we also had to show the number of units sold, quite clearly they cannot be plotted on the same numeric axis.

- ◆ The series use the same units but the magnitude of values differs. For example, in a chart showing monthly website traffic, if we also had to show the number of people completing a sale, the scale of the units for both of them would be very different.

All the previous cases require the use of **combination charts**. As the name suggests, they are either a combination of both comparison and transition chart types in the same chart, or have the same chart type but have multiple numeric axes, or both of them. Let us see what kind of combination chart is required for each of the cases mentioned previously.

Case 1: Combination chart with a single numeric axis

In a combination chart with a single numeric axis, all the data series have the same units and scale. So a single numeric axis works well for all the chart types the chart may have. The following screenshot shows how the 2011 monthly revenue chart would look with the 2010 values being used for individual comparison:

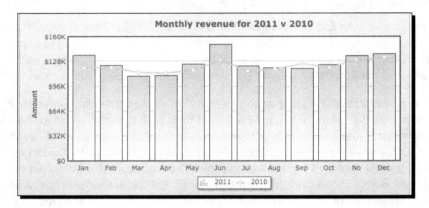

Notice how this is an improvement over both the multi-series column and line chart. As opposed to the column chart, the comparison analysis for the 2011 figures remains unhampered. Also, as compared to the line chart, finding out the exact difference in the revenue for, say, June, is much easier with the column serving as a backdrop. You can also use the area chart for plotting the 2010 values, but as we talked about earlier, when plotting multiple series, the line chart is a cleaner pick.

Case 2: Combination chart with dual numeric axes

In a combination chart with two numeric axes, each axis has its own unit and magnitude, and each data series conforms to one of these axes. Let us plot the sale of men's t-shirts in a store in terms of both revenue and units sold on one of these combination charts. We see a chart similar to the following screenshot:

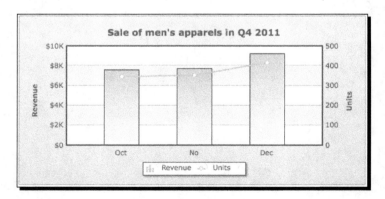

Case 3: Combination chart with dual numeric axes having the same units

Let's get back to the case where we have to plot the website traffic and the number of people closing the sale on the same chart. As the magnitude of the website traffic is much larger than the number of people checking out, the number of conversions will be completely squished.

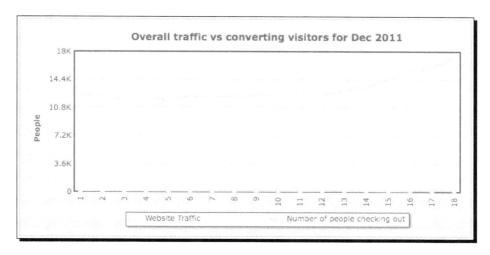

As we see in the previous screenshot, the number of people completing the conversion funnel is a straight line despite being in a pretty healthy zone of 100-200 daily. One way to get around the problem is to use a log axis so that the difference in the scale of magnitudes can be adjusted, as shown in the following screenshot:

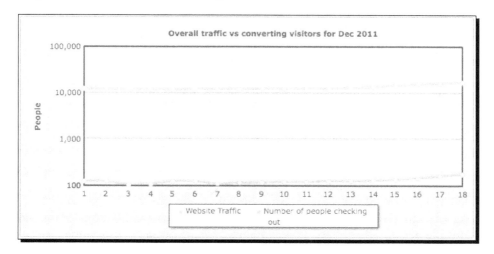

Charts having log axes are created for the very purpose of being able to plot data with a massive difference in scales. However, the fact remains that business users are much more used to the linear axis instead of the log axis. So you run the risk of them neglecting the log axis and interpreting completely different trends and patterns.

Let's stick with the linear axis and bring in a second y-axis to plot the number of conversions on it.

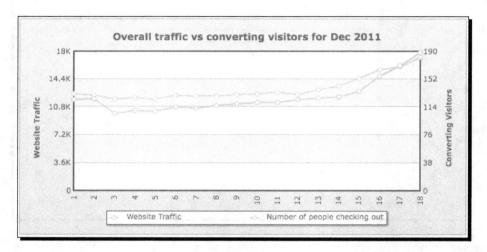

In the previous screenshot, see how everything gets sorted out just by bringing in another axis. The ratio of website traffic to converting visitors is stable throughout the month except at the end where there is a spike in the conversion, which could be because of improvements in the website experience or a wider variety of merchandise on offer for the holiday season. We used two line charts here to be able to see the ratio between the two data series better. However, you can use a combination of column and line or column charts on both axes depending on what analysis you want to facilitate.

Combination of comparison and composition charts

One of the first metrics that any business with an online arm looks at is the website traffic they generate. We have seen how to visualize this. To delve deeper into the traffic, they want to see how this traffic breaks down into different traffic sources—direct, search, or other referring sites. Again, this can be done with the help of a simple pie chart. But if the marketing manager wanted to analyze the traffic breakdown of all the twelve months in the year individually, creating twelve pie charts is definitely not the answer. And with different pie charts for each month, you wouldn't be able to compare the total traffic for the months either. This is when we need charts that combine comparison and composition charts. Say hello to the **stacked chart**. It is essentially a column chart with each column broken down into its respective constituents. The following screenshot shows how this would look for Harry's website:

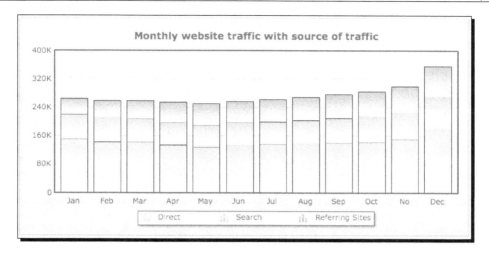

Very helpful, isn't it? You can compare the overall monthly traffic just as you could with a simple column chart, and see how the traffic for each month breaks down into direct, search, and referring sites. All of this within a single chart. You can also compare the direct traffic over 12 months. The only thing you cannot do is compare the traffic from search or referring sites over the months since they do not have a common base. But then, the reason for using the stacked chart was to compare the overall traffic and see how that breaks down into the constituents for each month. If you need to compare the constituents themselves over the months, the best way to go about is to create a separate column chart for each of the constituents.

Pop quiz – empowering your CEO

1. You need to make a dashboard for your CEO to show the revenue made every month for 2011. The chart should enable him to find the best performing month and also see the breakdown of each month's revenue into products and services. Which chart will you use?

   a. A multi-series column chart with one data series showing the product revenue in a month and another for services that appears right alongside the product figures every month

   b. A stacked column chart showing the total revenue for every month further broken down into products and services

Specialized charts

The charts for comparison, transition, and composition analysis take care of over two-thirds of the data analysis required in business applications. However, there are a number of metrics that can only be visualized with charts specialized for that purpose. We will take a look at these charts now.

Gauges

Gauges are single value indicators used to display **Key Performance Indicators (KPIs)** such as average sale per customer, conversion rates, current inventory levels, project status, and customer satisfaction index. The most commonly used gauge is the angular gauge, more popularly known as the speedometer chart. As the name implies, it is similar in both look and feel to the speedometer of a car. Let us plot the customer satisfaction rating for Harry's SuperMart on an angular gauge.

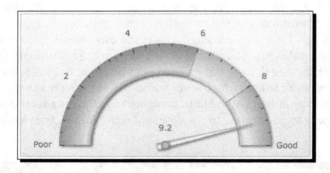

In the previous screenshot, the angular gauge shows the rating at 9.2 on a scale of 10. In addition to that, it also adds a lot of context to the data with the color range breaking down the complete scale into poor, moderate, and good. While you are free to choose any color you would like for the color ranges, it is best to stick to the universally accepted red for poor, yellow for moderate, and green for good performance.

Angular gauges are also used heavily in operational dashboards such as network and call center monitoring. In these cases, you will need the angular gauge to have the real-time capabilities that most vendors offer these days. The gauge will fetch new data from the server every *n* seconds, where *n* is the duration specified by you, and update automatically to show the new value.

You can also use the linear gauge and LED gauge for plotting KPIs. Similar to the angular gauge, as shown in the following screenshot, they allow you to add color ranges to the gauge to add more context to the data:

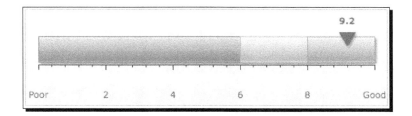

In the LED gauge, instead of using a pointer to mark out the value, the gauge itself stays lit till the point where the value is to be marked out, as shown in the following screenshot:

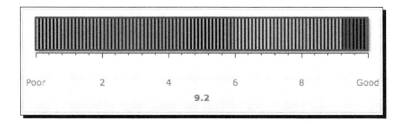

All the gauges we have seen till now are quantity indicators. Now we will look at a gauge that displays quantities in terms of qualitative signals—the bulb gauge. Used mostly in operational dashboards, the bulb gauge is a special gauge that is used to reflect a single state, using the universally understood red, yellow and green colors. For example, it can be used to monitor network usage in an organization and raise an alert by turning red when usage becomes too high.

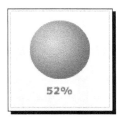

I can see the charts in FusionCharts XT but not the gauges. Where do I get them?

Gauges are a part of FusionWidgets XT which is a part of the FusionCharts Suite, and can be used individually as well. To learn how to implement the gauges for your application, head to http://docs.fusioncharts.com/widgets/. It is similar to the implementation of the color ranges we built for the maps.

Bullet graphs

The bullet graph is a variation of the bar chart designed by Stephen Few to replace gauges. Just like gauges, it is used to display a single indicator with color ranges adding context to the data. There are two important ways in which the bullet graph is different from gauges. Firstly, color ranges are variations of a single hue itself instead, with the lightest color standing for the best performance, unlike the red, yellow, and green colors used in a gauge. Secondly, you can compare the indicator you are plotting to a target or predicted value using a marker. The following screenshot shows how the customer satisfaction rating we had plotted on different gauges looks on a bullet graph.

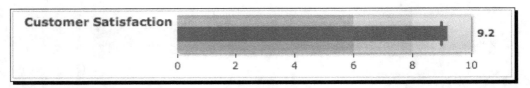

When compared to gauges, bullet graphs have the advantage of using less space and packing in more information with the marker. However, as a result of densely packing in information, quite often people have to spend more time interpreting data from a bullet graph than a gauge. This also results from the fact that people are much more used to gauges with their universally accepted colors than bullet graphs, which are relatively new and scarcely used in business visualizations. So the choice of which chart to use ultimately boils down to your audience's taste and knowledge. In case you are not sure, it is best to stick to the gauges.

The bullet graph is a part of FusionWidgets XT in the FusionCharts Suite.

Funnel chart

The funnel chart is used to show the **elimination of data** as it passes from one stage to another. Typical examples are sales conversion and recruitment funnels. In the sales conversion funnel, you start from the number of leads you have, move to the number of leads you could qualify, and finally the closure stage. Looking at the complete funnel, you can identify where the most leaks are happening and then get to work on that. Similarly, a recruitment funnel is used to understand the efficiency of the sourcing and screening process. The following screenshot shows how the recruitment funnel chart would look, should one of Harry's store manager decide to review his hiring numbers:

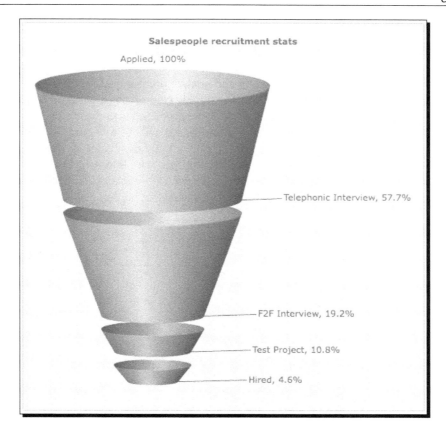

In the previous screenshot, the funnel shows numbers from the process as it streamlines from the start to the end with the bottom of the funnel showing the numbers at the end of the process.

 The funnel chart is also a part of FusionWidgets XT in the FusionCharts Suite.

Editable charts

Editable charts are essentially interactive forms of the conventional column and line charts, using which, the end user can visually edit the values in the chart. They are used as **interactive planning tools** by allowing the user to set up and analyze different what-if scenarios on the chart. For example, let's say Harry was given an editable column chart with the annual revenue for five years—three historical (noneditable), and two predicted values (editable). During one of his boardroom meetings, Harry gets ambitious and decides to increase the prediction set for next year. An effective planning tool should show him how his region and category-wise revenue have to increase to be able to achieve the glory he is looking for. This has to be done by intelligently tying the editable chart to other metrics in the backend. The following screenshot shows the editable column chart Harry will have at his disposal:

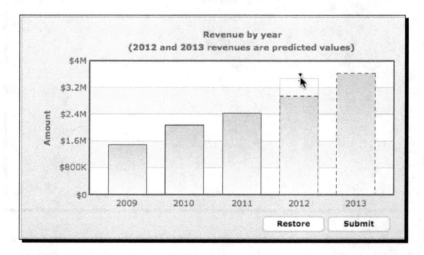

Not too many vendors offer editable charts, but FusionCharts Suite offers editable versions of column, line, and area charts. The charts when used correctly can be a very powerful and modern tool in the hands of executives.

 The editable charts are a part of PowerCharts in the FusionCharts Suite.

Gantt chart

The Gantt chart is a specialized chart developed by Henry Gantt used for planning and scheduling projects. It is used to lay out the order in which tasks need to be carried out, manage dependencies between them, and determine the resources needed. So if Harry's Marketing manager had to go about planning a marketing campaign for the holiday season, his Gantt chart would look similar to the following screenshot:

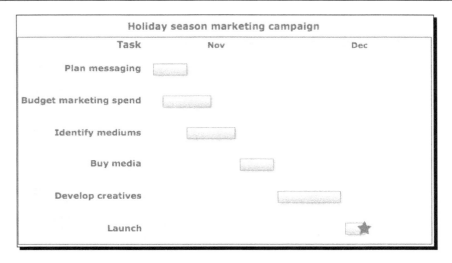

As you can see, the tasks involved in the project are listed out on the left with the time period on the right. You can break down the time period further into weeks and days, if needed. Then you put dates to the tasks involved, which can be dependent on the completion of the previous task or can be started independently. Finally, you mark out the completion of important phases of the project as milestones, which are typically indicated using stars.

You can also use the Gantt chart to see the progress of the project till date.

In the previous screenshot, the filled bars indicate the tasks that have been completed while the empty ones indicate work that is yet to be done.

The Gantt chart is thus a great aid for planning the workings of a project and managing the resources involved.

 The Gantt Chart is a part of FusionWidgets XT in the FusionCharts Suite.

Heat map chart

The heat map chart is a tabular representation of data with user-defined color ranges such as poor, moderate, and high. It is used to analyze complex data such as stock market investments, network utilization rates, and performance comparison of companies. If one of Harry's regional managers had to compare a number of stores under him on various factors to identify the areas of improvement, the heat map chart would look similar to the following screenshot:

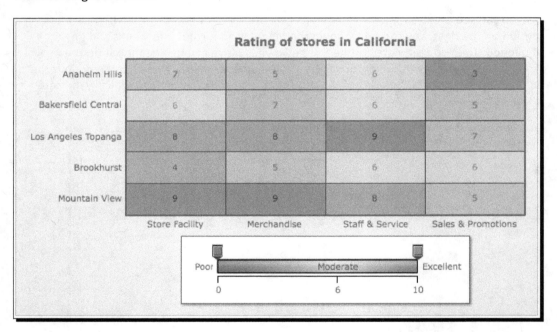

Quite clearly, the **Mountain View** store is the highest rated store in the region, and **Sales & Promotions** is something that needs to be worked on. For other stores or factors as well, it is much easier to identify the good and the bad points than if simply represented in a tabular format.

With an interactive heat map chart, the analysis can become one step easier. Let's say the manager wants to focus on only the factors and the stores that are of concern. In the legend, he can select the range he wants to focus on, say 0 to 6, and all other data sets will vanish from view, as shown in the following screenshot:

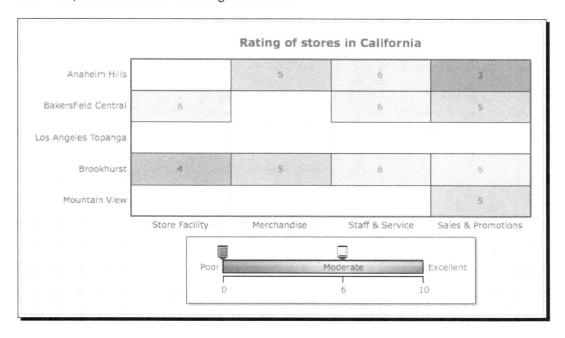

The heat map chart can thus be a very powerful tool in the hands of an end user for analyzing two-dimensional data.

 The heat map chart is a part of PowerCharts in the FusionCharts Suite.

Pop quiz – know thy heat map

1. Which of the following is not an ideal candidate for the heat map chart?

    a. Network utilization rate by the hour

    b. Revenue from different product categories for Q1-Q4 2011

    c. Conversion rate of different marketing mediums for Jan-Dec 2011

XY chart

The XY chart, also known as a scatter plot, is a mathematical diagram used to understand the **relationship** between two variables. Common examples include understanding the variation of weight with height, rainfall with temperature, server load with response time, and income with spend. An important thing to note is that both axes in an XY chart are numeric, whereas all other charts have one numeric axis and one category axis (including time-based categories).

In an XY chart, typically there is one independent variable and one dependent variable with the independent variable being plotted on the x-axis and the corresponding values of the dependent variable on the y-axis. Both these values combine into a single point that can be anywhere on the chart. If there is no dependent variable, the variables can be plotted along any axis. The following screenshot shows a market research example in which people were surveyed to find out how their incomes and spend on LCD TV were related:

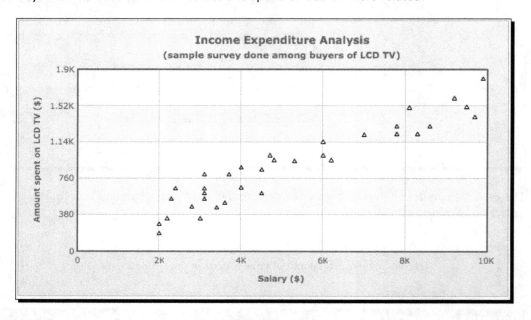

As expected, as salary goes up, so does the amount spent on LCD TV. This is called a **positive correlation** between the two variables. Similarly two variables can also have a negative correlation or have no correlation whatsoever, in which case the dots will be scattered all over the chart.

To understand the trend of the y-axis values with respect to the x-axis values better, regression lines are also used. They are displayed in a straight line that can be used to predict future values such as sales, commodity prices, productivity gains from a training program, and similar. So if we had to see the trend of spend on LCD TV with relation to the buyer's salary, it would look similar to the following screenshot:

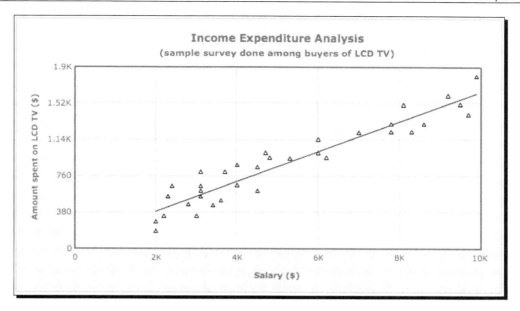

 The XY chart is a part of FusionCharts XT in the FusionCharts Suite.

Summary

Every business today has a lot of data. It is only through visualizing it correctly that it can be converted into powerful actionable information which is what we learned in this chapter. Specifically, we learned:

- How to understand who our dashboard is meant for and the metrics that interest them
- Common types of data analysis including comparison, composition, and transition
- Combining multiple forms of analysis into a single chart in combination and stacked chart
- The use of charts such as gauges, funnel chart, and Gantt chart for specialized applications

In the next and final chapter of the book, we will learn how to increase the usability of our charts and make it easier for the audience to understand them.

9
Increasing the Usability of your Charts

People are getting busier and busier every day. In a bid to do more in less time, they want to see and do things in the quickest and easiest possible way. They want to get started without having to read any help docs and manuals. They want to avoid errors and mistakes to be more efficient with their time. As such, usability has become a necessary condition for survival for business applications, both external and internal. If it's an external application, more usable applications mean more customers, and if it's internal, then it is a matter of employee productivity and overall buy-in to the system.

Charts can be made more usable using simple tips and techniques. This leads to quicker comprehension of the data on the chart, and also makes sure that people see and absorb everything that you are trying to convey with the chart.

In this chapter, we shall learn how to:

- Convey what the chart is for, clearly and succinctly
- Make charts more meaningful by adding context to the data
- De-clutter charts having excessive details

The chapter takes you through nine simple usability tips that can be applied to a majority of business scenarios.

Use descriptive captions

The caption of a chart should describe what the chart is completely about. In a chart showing the website traffic for a particular time period, the caption should clearly mention the purpose of the chart along with the time period for which the data is being displayed, as shown in the following screenshot:

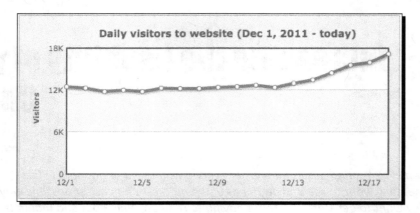

The caption should also mention the scale and the units of the numbers on the chart, if any. In fact, the caption should be so descriptive that the axes titles, if used, are only present as reinforcements.

However, with so many details in the caption, it might be difficult to accommodate everything in one line. That is when the subcaption comes into play. Typically, the units and scale of the numbers on the chart are delegated to the subcaption and so are details of lesser importance, as shown in the following screenshot:

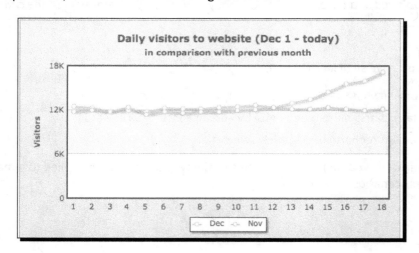

Arrange data whenever possible

As we saw in the previous chapter, whenever the data in the chart does not have to follow a time-based or alphabetical sequence, arranging the data in ascending or descending order makes data analysis a lot easier.

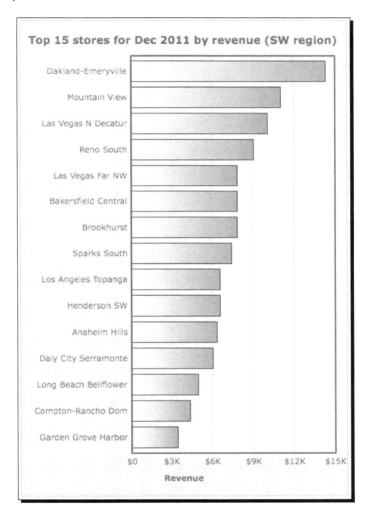

As our aim was to find the highest selling store in Dec 2011, arranging the data in descending order was the obvious choice, as shown in the previous screenshot. Choosing the order follows naturally from the purpose of the chart.

Arranging data is not limited to column and bar charts only. It can be quite helpful in pie charts as well. Let's say you had a pie chart showing the breakdown of revenue from different countries for 2011, as displayed in the following screenshot:

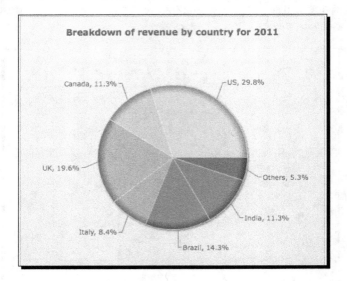

While it is easy to see that US brought in the most revenue in 2011, finding out the second and the third best countries does require a fair amount of looking around. This can be made much easier by simply arranging the data, as in the following screenshot:

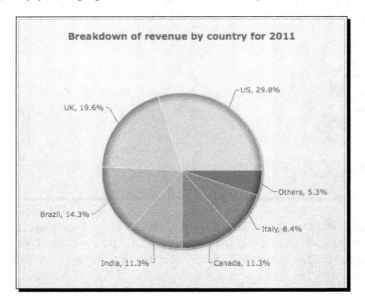

Delegate detailed info to tooltips

Capabilities such as tooltips and drill-down are what make interactive charts much more useful than Excel-type images. In an image, all the information associated with a chart has to go on the chart itself. Quite often, this results in the chart getting cluttered with excessive details. to prevent that, the details are crimped. However, with interactive charts, all the detailed information can go in the tooltip. So in a chart showing daily footfall at a store, the explanation for why there was a sudden increase or decrease in the number of visitors can easily go in the tooltip, as shown in the following screenshot:

By putting the details in the tooltips, the chart stays clean and the user has all the required details at his disposal. However, how does the user know that he can get more info by hovering over a data point, or clicking on tablets and smartphones? The points with more details on them can be highlighted and we can add a simple message in the sub-caption indicating that the highlighted points have tooltips, as displayed in the following screenshot:

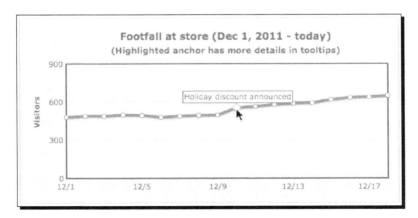

Mention the chart has drill-down

Just like with tooltips, if the chart drills down to a more detailed level, there is no way for the user to know. So it is important to mention that the chart has drill-down. Again, the sub-caption is a good place to put this, as shown in the following screenshot:

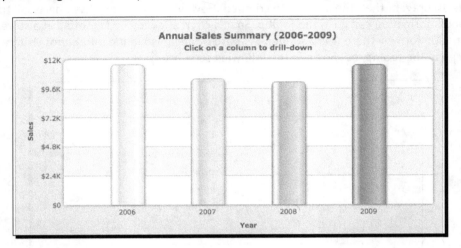

Add context to data using trendlines

If you are plotting monthly revenue from a particular store for a year, wouldn't it make more sense to the viewer to see what the target was as well? Or last month's average on a chart showing daily footfall at the store? By displaying targets, predictions, or average from a previous time period, we add more context to data. This allows the user to see if the sales for the month met the target or if the daily footfall was good at the store. The addition of context to the chart is done using trendlines.

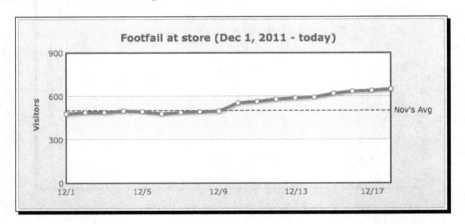

In the previous screenshot, just by adding the trendlines, it is clear that the footfall is in line with November's average and once the holiday season kicks in, it is all upwards from there on.

Remove excess precision from data

If you are plotting an annual revenue chart, as in the following screenshot, talking about millions of dollars every month, then showing the 24 Cents at the end of the figures is of no use.

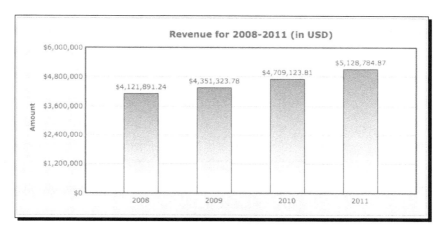

This typically happens when the value is directly pulled from the database and plotted on the chart. Just by rounding off the numbers to the nearest hundredth or thousandth, as shown in the following screenshot, the figures become so much easier to understand.

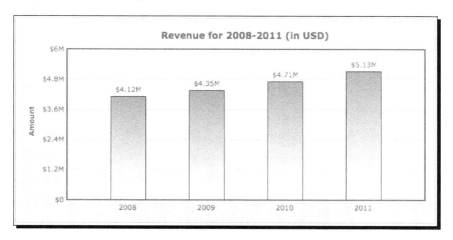

Show predicted values using a dashed border

Many times, during sales forecasting or project planning, you need to show predicted values on the chart. To make sure the user doesn't mix up the known and the predicted values when he is deep in his analysis, it is best to show predicted values using a dashed border, as shown in the following screenshot:

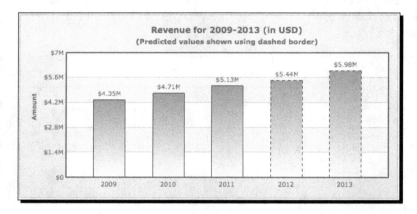

Dashed borders are often used to highlight a data set as well, but with a small note in the subcaption, you can be sure to eliminate the confusion.

Start the y-axis at zero at all times

In the previous annual revenue chart, as all the values are between **$4M-$6M**, it might be tempting to bring out the difference better by starting the y-axis at say, **$4M**. Let's see how that works out.

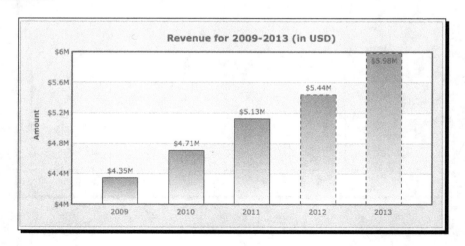

In the previous screenshot, looking at the columns, it looks like revenue has been doubling every year since 2009 and that's how it's predicted to go for 2012 and 2013 as well. However, this misinterpretation is because we started the y-axis at **$4M** instead of zero. Any time you do this, the chart is going to tell a different story than the underlying data. So make sure to start the numeric axis at zero for all composition and transition charts.

Use vertical separators when plotting data for irregular intervals

Say you have to plot monthly footfall at a store for a pretty irregular interval, Aug 2010 to Apr 2011. Users are typically used to seeing monthly data for 12 months one after another or quarterly data for the four quarters, but surely not data from Aug 2010 to Apr 2011.

Typically, the dynamics from one calendar year to another change a lot. To make sure that the user knows when 2010 ends and when 2011 starts, even when he is deeply immersed in his data analysis, put a vertical separator line between 2010 and 2011, as shown in the following screenshot:

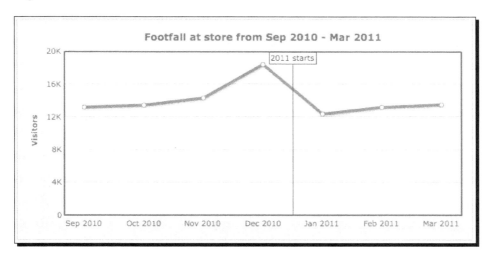

Summary

In this chapter, we saw how with a little attention to details, we can make the chart much more usable for our audience. Specifically we covered:

◆ How to explain the purpose of the chart completely using the caption and subcaption

◆ How to make the chart easier to comprehend by arranging the data, using dashed borders for predicted values, and using a vertical line when plotting data for irregular intervals

◆ How to add more value to the chart using trendlines and detailed tooltips

◆ Avoid mistakes in a chart; always mention if the chart has drill-down and start the y-axis from zero

That's it. Now you are fully equipped to go ahead and create delightful charts for yourself and your organization. Not only do you know how to give a face to your data, but you also know how to select the right face for it and make it most usable for your users, something a lot of developers fall short on. Go ahead and wow the world.

All the best!

Pop Quiz Answers

Chapter 3: JavaScript Capabilities

Know your chart object

Question Number	Answer
1	b

Know when to use the advanced event model

Question Number	Answer
1	c

Do you recall the JSON data API?

Question Number	Answer
1	c

Chapter 5: Exporting Charts

Know the possibilities

Question Number	Answer
1	JPEG image, PNG image and PDF document
2	c
3	`exportEnabled="1"`, `exportAtClient="1"` and `export Handler="YourExportComponentID"`

JavaScript Export API

Question Number	Answer
1	`exportChart()`
2	`exportFileName`
3	`ExportReady`

Chapter 8: Selecting the Right Visualization for your Data

Know your dashboard audience

Question Number	Answer
1	a

Empowering your CEO

Question Number	Answer
1	a

Know thy heat map

Question Number	Answer
1	b. The color range defined in the heat map chart is common for all the categories. So, it is ideal for plotting data where all the categories are normalized on the same scale, such as percentages and rating scale. When plotting revenues from different product categories, the range for poor and good sales will be different for various categories, and defining a common range will result in a misrepresentation of data.

Index

button, creating for 122-124
  enabling, context-menu used 114-119
charts, exporting as image
  buttons, creating for 125-128
charts, exporting as PDF
  buttons, creating for 125-128
charts export parameters
  configuring, JavaScript used 125
Charts folder 11
charts, modes
  auto 59
  rotate 58
  skip 59
  stagger 59
  wrap 58
child chart. *See* **descendant chart**
client-side
  charts, exporting at 114
Code folder 11
color
  customizing, of data plots 51, 52
color attribute 51
Column 2D chart 26
combination charts
  about 39
  actual, versus projected revenue 40, 41
  dual Y-axes combination charts 39
  revenue, versus units sold 42-44
  single Y-axis combination charts 39
  with dual numeric axes 198
  with dual numeric axes having same units 199, 200
  with single numeric axis 198
compact constructor method 22
comparison analysis 189, 191
comparison charts
  combining, with composition charts 200
  combining, with transition charts 197
composition analysis 194
composition charts
  combining, with comparison charts 200
configuring
  legend, in multi-series charts 61
  server-side export handler 129
  tooltips 60
connectToDB() function 145

context
  adding, to data with trendlines 218, 219
context menu
  used, for enabling charts export 114-119
Core FusionCharts files 11
CSV format
  chart data, retrieving as 85-87
currency notes
  setting, as background charts 49, 50
custom labels
  used, for adding details to charts 60

D

dashboard
  about 8
  building 26
dashboard audience
  about 188, 189
  operational users 188
  strategic users 188
  tactical users 188
dashed border
  used, for displaying predicted values 220
data
  arranging 215, 216
  excess precision, removing from 219
  plotting, at irregular intervals with vertical separators 221
  providing, Data String method used 26
  retrieving, from charts 82-85
data analysis
  multiple forms, combining 195-197
  types 189
data analysis, types
  about 189
  comparison 189-191
  composition 194
  transition 192-194
data labels
  about 57
  customizing 58, 59
data plots
  about 47, 96
  border, customizing 52
  color, customizing for 51, 52
  customizing 51

F

rotate mode, for charts 58

S

script
  used, for writing BOM stamp 66
sender variable 77
server
  charts, exporting to 128
server-side chart export
  performing, button used 130-133
server-side export handler
  configuring 129
server-side scripts
  and FusionCharts 136
setChartAttribute function 89
setJSONData() method 28, 31, 33, 80, 137
setJSONUrl() method 28, 31, 80, 137
setXMLData() function 32, 80
setXMLData() method 26, 137
setXMLUrl() method 26, 36, 80
setXMLURL() method 137
Shockwave (SWF) 10
showExportDialog property 127
showExportUrl function 133
simple event model
  about 73-75
  charts controls, displaying 73-75
simple events
  replacing, with advanced event model 76
single XML source
  used, for creating LinkedCharts 107-110
single Y-axis combination charts 39
skip mode, for charts 59
sortData function 84, 86
sort method 85
SourceCode folder 11
specialized charts
  about 202
  bullet graph 204
  editable charts 206
  funnel chart 204, 205
  Gantt chart 206, 207
  gauges 202, 203
  heat map chart 208, 209

XY chart 210, 211
stacked chart 200
stagger mode, for charts 59
statusCode property 133
statusMessage property 133
stopPropagation() method 77
strategic users 188

T

tactical users 188
target revenue
  displaying, trendline used 62, 63
Tools folder 11
tooltips
  about 217
  configuring 60
  detailed info, delegating to 217
transition analysis 192-194
transition charts
  combining, with combining charts 197
  combining, with comparison charts 197
trendline
  about 62
  adding, to charts 62
  used, for adding context to data 218, 219
  used, for displaying target revenue 62, 63
trendzones
  about 63
  adding, to charts 63

U

updateChartCosmetics function 89
updateData function 80, 82

V

version
  upgrading, for FusionCharts 16
Version.txt file 11
vertical separators
  used, for plotting data at irregular intervals 221
vMargin attribute 121

W

web page
  XML, embedding in 26-28
web pages
  FusionCharts, embedding in 136
width attribute 121
width property 133
wrap mode, for charts 58

X

XML
  embedding, in web page 26-28
  special characters, encoding 18

XML data
  creating, for chart 17, 18
  creating, for map 177, 178
XMLGenerator 11
XMLLoadingText attribute 66
XML relayer script file
  BOM stamp, adding to 66
XY chart 210, 211

Y

y-axis
  customizing 53-55
  starting, at all times 220, 221

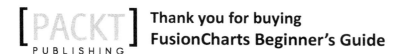

About Packt Publishing

Packt, pronounced 'packed', published its first book "Mastering phpMyAdmin for Effective MySQL Management" in April 2004 and subsequently continued to specialize in publishing highly focused books on specific technologies and solutions.

Our books and publications share the experiences of your fellow IT professionals in adapting and customizing today's systems, applications, and frameworks. Our solution-based books give you the knowledge and power to customize the software and technologies you're using to get the job done. Packt books are more specific and less general than the IT books you have seen in the past. Our unique business model allows us to bring you more focused information, giving you more of what you need to know, and less of what you don't.

Packt is a modern, yet unique publishing company, which focuses on producing quality, cutting-edge books for communities of developers, administrators, and newbies alike. For more information, please visit our website: www.PacktPub.com.

Writing for Packt

We welcome all inquiries from people who are interested in authoring. Book proposals should be sent to author@packtpub.com. If your book idea is still at an early stage and you would like to discuss it first before writing a formal book proposal, contact us; one of our commissioning editors will get in touch with you.

We're not just looking for published authors; if you have strong technical skills but no writing experience, our experienced editors can help you develop a writing career, or simply get some additional reward for your expertise.

jQuery 1.4 Reference Guide

ISBN: 978-1-849510-04-2   Paperback: 336 pages

A comprehensive exploration of the popular
JavaScript library

1. Quickly look up features of the jQuery library

2. Step through each function, method, and
   selector expression in the jQuery library with an
   easy-to-follow approach

3. Understand the anatomy of a jQuery script

4. Write your own plug-ins using jQuery's powerful
   plug-in architecture

5. Written by the creators of learningquery.com

Alfresco Share

ISBN: 978-1-84951-710-2   Paperback: 360 pages

Enterprise Collaboration and Efficient Social
Content Management

1. Understand the concepts and benefits of Share

2. Leverage a single installation to manage
   multiple sites

3. Case Study-based approach for effective
   understanding

Please check **www.PacktPub.com** for information on our titles

Flash iOS Apps Cookbook

ISBN: 978-1-84969-138-3   Paperback: 420 pages

100 practical recipes for developing iOS apps with Flash Professional and Adobe AIR

1. Build your own apps, port existing projects, and learn the best practices for targeting iOS devices using Flash.

2. How to compile a native iOS app directly from Flash and deploy it to the iPhone, iPad or iPod touch.

3. Full of practical recipes and step-by-step instructions for developing iOS apps with Flash Professional.

Flash 10 Multiplayer Game Essentials

ISBN: 978-1-847196-60-6   Paperback: 336 pages

Create exciting real-time multiplayer games using Flash

1. A complete end-to-end guide for creating fully featured multiplayer games

2. The author's experience in the gaming industry enables him to share insights on multiplayer game development

3. Walk-though several real-time multiplayer game implementations

4. Packed with illustrations and code snippets with supporting explanations for ease of understanding

Please check **www.PacktPub.com** for information on our titles

www.ingramcontent.com/pod-product-compliance
Lightning Source LLC
LaVergne TN
LVHW062312060326
832902LV00013B/2173